D1370316

ZIMBABWE
in Pictures

Francesca Di Piazza

Lerner Publications Company

Contents

Lerner Publishing Group realizes that current information and statistics quickly become out of date. To extend the usefulness of the Visual Geography Series, we developed www.vgsbooks.com, a website offering links to up-to-date information, as well as in-depth material, on a wide variety of subjects. All of the websites listed on www.vgsbooks.com have been carefully selected by researchers at Lerner Publishing Group. However, Lerner Publishing Group is not responsible for the accuracy or suitability of the material on any website other than <www.lernerbooks.com>. It is recommended that students using the Internet be supervised by a parent or teacher. Links on www.vgsbooks.com will be regularly reviewed and updated as needed.

Website address: www.lernerbooks.com

Lerner Publications Company
A division of Lerner Publishing Group
241 First Avenue North
Minneapolis, MN 55401 U.S.A.

web enhanced @ www.vgsbooks.com

CULTURAL LIFE   46

▶ Pieces of the Past. Shona Sculpture and Art in
Life. Literature, Drama, and Film. Music and Dance.
Religion. Sports and Recreation. Food.

THE ECONOMY   58

▶ Land Resettlement. Agriculture and Forestry.
Industry, Manufacturing, and Mining. Service
Sector. Hydroelectric Power and Fuel. Foreign
Debt, Black Market, and Crime. The Future.

FOR MORE INFORMATION

Library of Congress Cataloging-in-Publication Data

Di Piazza, Francesca.
      Zimbabwe in pictures / by Francesca Di Piazza.
        p.   cm. — (Visual geography series)
      Includes bibliographical references and index.
      ISBN: 0-8225-2399-X (lib. bdg. : alk. paper)
       1. Zimbabwe—Pictorial works—Juvenile literature. 2. Zimbabwe—Juvenile literature. I. Title. II. Series.
    DT2893.05 2005
    968.91'0022'2—dc22   2004017905

Manufactured in the United States of America
1 2 3 4 5 6 - BP - 10 09 08 07 06 05

INTRODUCTION

"You have given me the jewel of Africa." The man who spoke these words on the eve of his nation's independence in 1980 was Robert Mugabe, a leader in Zimbabwe's struggle for independence. He was about to be made the new nation's first prime minister. The man he spoke them to was Prime Minister Ian Smith, the outgoing representative of white minority rule. The country they were discussing was Zimbabwe, once called Rhodesia, a land in southern Africa that had just emerged from civil war.

Zimbabwe is a jewel because it is rich in resources. A rocky ridge called the Great Dike runs the length of the country. In these hills are many minerals, including emeralds, and precious metals, including gold. Other minerals bring the country export income and provide raw materials for manufacturing and industry. Other riches include the country's fertile grasslands and the forested mountains of its Eastern Highlands. Blessed with a mild climate, the land will grow almost anything. Zimbabwe has been one of the world's leading

tobacco growers. It also exports flowers and fruits. Gorgeous granite landscapes in the western part of the country are home to some of the best safari and wildlife parks in Africa. The rivers that form the country's northern and southern borders, the Zambezi and Limpopo, respectively, provide irrigation and hydroelectric power and link the landlocked nation with the Indian Ocean to the east. Thunderous Victoria Falls on the Zambezi River is one of the seven natural wonders of the world.

The history of Zimbabwe runs deep and long. Ancient rock paintings are evidence of hunter-gatherers who lived in the area many thousands of years ago. Starting in the tenth century A.D., merchants established trade routes linking the region to the Indian Ocean coast. In the twentieth century, the new republic took its name from the ruins of fifteenth century Great Zimbabwe (meaning "great stone houses"), which lie near Masvingo. In choosing a name from the Shona language—one of Zimbabwe's main tongues—Zimbabwe proudly

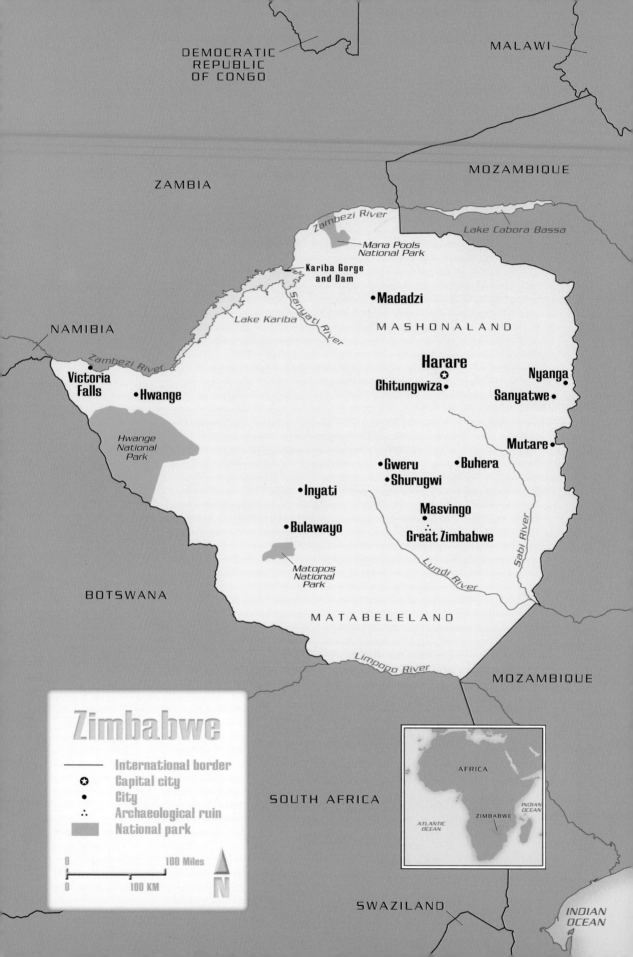

proclaimed its ties to centuries of African achievement. The Ndebele (en-deh-BEL-lay), Zimbabwe's second largest ethnic group after the Shona, arrived in the area in the early nineteenth century. The territory was dubbed Rhodesia—after the British financier Cecil Rhodes—by its white, colonial population, who arrived in the late nineteenth century. The arrival of white settlers, who seized the best land, led to more than eighty years of rule by the white minority and political and social inequality for the black people. Starting in the late 1960s, a guerrilla (nontraditional) war was waged, and majority rule and full independence was finally achieved in 1980.

Independence brought high hopes to Zimbabwe. Despite years of division, people pulled together to create equal opportunities for all. Prime Minister Mugabe set the tone by calling for peace, unity, and forgiveness. Within a few years, however, the country was facing a decline.

Mugabe's government gradually became more autocratic (ruled by one person with unlimited authority) and less democratic. Government-sponsored seizure of commercial farms from white farmers started in the year 2000. Zimbabwe had once been a big exporter of food to other parts of southern Africa, but ongoing violence over land ownership coupled with drought has devastated agriculture to the point where many in the nation face famine. In 2002 international observers called that year's presidential elections corrupt and unfair. In the early twenty-first century, government mismanagement of the economy has led to international isolation, an unemployment rate of 70 percent, and constantly increasing inflation. These factors are made more challenging by the presence of the human immunodeficiency virus (HIV), the virus that often causes the deadly disease acquired immunodeficiency syndrome (AIDS). Africa has been hard hit by HIV/AIDS, and Zimbabwe has the fourth highest infection rate in the world.

THE LAND

The landlocked Republic of Zimbabwe lies in southern Africa. It is part of the region south of the Zambezi River known as Southern Africa, which includes six other countries—Namibia, Botswana, South Africa, Lesotho, Swaziland, and Mozambique. Zimbabwe's area of 150,820 square miles (390,624 square kilometers) makes it nearly as large as California. The boundaries of Zimbabwe generally lie where natural barriers exist. To the north, the Zambezi River separates Zimbabwe from Zambia and Namibia. The Limpopo River forms Zimbabwe's southern boundary with neighboring Botswana and South Africa. Mozambique's border lies to the east and north of Zimbabwe, along the path of the Eastern Highlands.

◉ The Plains

A great plateau (raised, flat land) dominates southern Africa. The central part of Zimbabwe's section of this plateau is a plain (flat, mostly treeless land). It is called the Highveld (*veld* means "plain"

in Afrikaans, a language developed in Africa from Dutch). This plain stretches 400 miles (644 km) north to south and 50 miles (80 km) west to east. Stony hills called kopjes occasionally rise up out of the flat landscape. A ridge of low hills called the Great Dike runs through the center of the plain from northeast to southwest. The Great Dike is rich in minerals, including gold, silver, and platinum. With its pleasant climate, grassy plains, and areas of woodland, the Highveld provides conditions suitable for herding and farming. Zimbabwe's main cities and commercial farms are situated on the Highveld. Farmers can be hard hit by recurring drought, though, and the soil ranges from very fertile to very poor.

On either side of the Highveld, the Middleveld slopes downward from an elevation of 4,000 to 2,000 feet (1,219 to 619 meters) above sea level. Rivers flow down from the plateau, and deep river valleys split this area into great expanses of grasslands. The rivers carve through hard rocks that contain gold, washing the gold into the water. Many Zimbabweans pan for gold in these rivers. Because most of the Middleveld slants downhill and much of its poor topsoil has been washed away by rains, it is not well suited for growing crops. Cattle herding has been central to the life of the people there for hundreds of years.

The Lowveld, which is less than 2,000 feet (619 m) above sea level, consists of a narrow strip of land in the Zambezi Valley and a broader tract between the Limpopo and Sabi rivers to the south. The scrubby landscape of the Lowveld is dotted with giant granite boulders. The dry soil in the Lowveld is not fertile, and erosion from heavy rains makes farming crops difficult. In the hot, wet lowland summers, mosquitoes carrying malaria are a danger to people. Tsetse flies carry sleeping sickness, a deadly disease that threatens cattle. The insects have been partly overcome, but cattle herders still practice transhumance (the seasonal movement of livestock), moving their cattle into higher grazing lands in the summer to avoid disease.

One of Africa's best game preserves, Hwange National Park, lies in the west. It encompasses segments of both the Lowveld and the Middlevelt regions of Zimbabwe. The area is sparsely populated.

The Eastern Highlands

Along Zimbabwe's eastern border with Mozambique lies a belt of mountain ranges collectively called the Eastern Highlands. Open, rolling grasslands between the mountains are broken up by forests and by coffee, fruit, and flower farms. The highlands not only form a natural boundary but are also a major watershed, or drainage area, for the region's rivers and streams.

The misty, forested peaks of the Vumba Mountains—located in the center of this long highland belt—rise to several thousand feet in height. To the north of this range are the Inyanga Mountains, where Mount Inyangani—Zimbabwe's highest point—rises to 8,514 feet (2,595 m).

◐ Rivers

Two rivers flow along Zimbabwe's northern and southern borders— the Zambezi and the Limpopo, respectively. The Zambezi, Africa's fourth longest river, flows east from Zambia through Lake Kariba, which was created by the Kariba Dam at the Kariba Gorge. The river eventually runs into the Mozambique Channel and empties into the Indian Ocean to the east. Within Zimbabwe, the Sanyati River flows into the Zambezi and drains the interior of the country.

The Limpopo travels east along Zimbabwe's southern border, forming the entire border with South Africa. This river, sometimes called the Crocodile, flows across Mozambique and into the Indian Ocean. The Sabi and Lundi rivers water south-central regions of Zimbabwe. From the Highveld, each flows southeastward toward Mozambique. The lowest point in Zimbabwe—only 531 feet (162 m) above sea level—is where the Sabi and Lundi rivers meet near the Mozambique border.

A blazing sun sets over the **Zambezi River** in northern Zimbabwe.

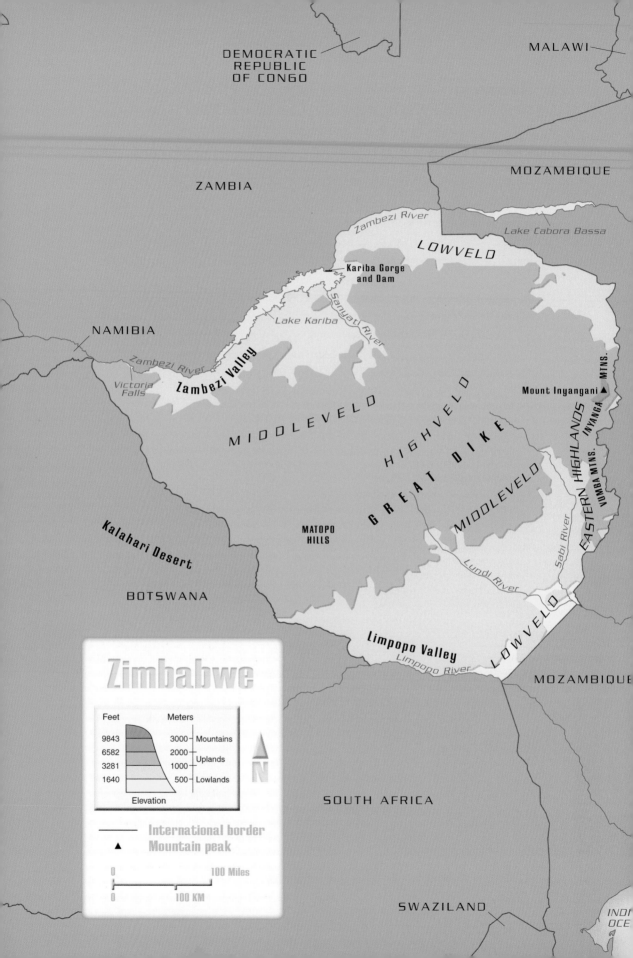

◉ Victoria Falls

When the Zambezi River reaches Victoria Falls, the waterway is 1.3 miles (2 km) wide. Its powerful volume of water hurtles down a 350-foot (107 m) chasm (crack in the earth's surface) with a thunderous roar and sends smokelike spray 1,500 feet (457 m) into the air. The spray is visible from miles away. During times of flooding, the local name for the falls—Mosi-oa-Tunya, meaning "smoke that thunders"— is especially fitting. At its peak, 132 million gallons (600 million liters) of water crash over the falls each minute. These magnificent falls on the border with Zambia to the northwest form one of the most impressive sights in all of Africa.

◉ Kariba Dam and Lake Kariba

The Kariba Dam was built on the Zambezi River some distance below Victoria Falls. It was constructed in the 1950s to provide hydroelectric power for industry. The name Kariba comes from the Shona word *kariwa,* meaning "a little trap," and refers to the narrowing of the Zambezi River at the Kariba Gorge.

The **Kariba Dam** is located in an active earthquake zone. Since its completion in 1959, more than twenty earthquakes strong enough to cause damage have been recorded.

Herds of elephants and antelope *(above)* regularly visit **Lake Kariba** in their migratory searches for food and water. "A land without animals is a dead land," according to Zimbabwe's indigenous Shangaan people.

The dam formed Lake Kariba, one of the largest artificial lakes in the world, covering 2,050 square miles (5,309 sq. km). When the land was flooded, fifty-seven thousand indigenous (local) Tonga people were displaced and resettled on higher ground. Lake Kariba—which is 175 miles (282 km) long and 20 miles (32 km) across at its widest point—is in the heart of a fertile region. Many animals and birds live on the shores of the lake. Jellyfish, plankton, and shrimp live in the lake, and gulls, terns, and eagles fly overhead and dive for fish.

As the Zambezi River began to flood the land upstream from the completed Kariba Dam, Operation Noah swung into action. People from all over the world sent vast sums of money to help rescue more than six thousand animals from the rising water. Smaller animals were caught in nets and transported by boat to dry land. Elephants and other large animals were herded into the water and assisted in their long swim ashore.

◉ Flora and Fauna

Large numbers of elephants, lions, monkeys, hippopotamuses, zebras, giraffes, buffalo, and antelope are found mainly in Zimbabwe's national parks. Close to two hundred species of mammals, including hyenas, cheetahs, leopards, and numerous varieties of deer, also live in Zimbabwe. The honey badger is a carnivore (meat eater) that eats bee brood (young bees developing in the hive), not honey. This fierce hunter will kill and eat poisonous snakes and even small crocodiles. Many endangered species, such as the rhinoceros, the aardwolf (related to the hyena), and the pangolin—or scaly anteater—are given special protection.

Zimbabwe is also home to a large number and variety of birds. For example, there are eight species of robins, eleven kinds of cuckoos, and seventeen different eagles. Brightly feathered birds include redbreasted shrikes, green and purple lories, and bee-eaters. Songbirds such as warblers, canaries, and finches enliven the air with their pleasant calls. Birds migrate to the country's rivers and woodlands from Europe, Asia, and neighboring African lands. More than five hundred kinds of butterflies add color to the air.

Numerous game parks have been established both to conserve animal life and to provide a means of viewing the creatures in their native habitats. More than 3 million acres (1.2 million hectares) of the country have been declared national parks and wildlife reserves.

Zimbabwe's lakes and rivers are home to 131 species of fish. Reptiles are well represented in Zimbabwe. The nation has 76 species

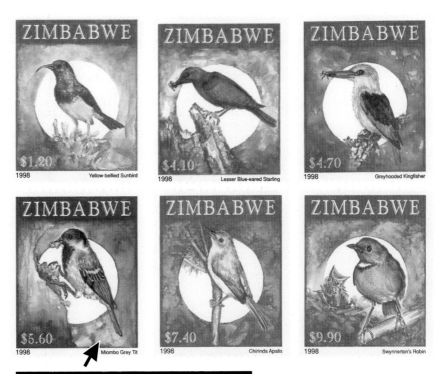

A wide variety of birds found in Zimbabwe appears on the nation's postage stamps. Go to www.vgsbooks.com for links about Zimbabwe's wildlife.

of snakes, including the python, which grows to 16 feet (5 m) in length. This giant snake kills small mammals by squeezing them until they suffocate. Deadly poisonous snakes include the gaboon viper, puff adder, and four kinds of cobras. Crocodiles, tortoises, and many kinds of lizards, including the 6-foot (2-m) long monitor lizard, are found in the country.

Zimbabwe's climate allows for a wide variety of cultivated flowers and fruits, ranging from roses to bananas. Most of the land is grassland, with thorny acacia trees and dry, open woodlands. Msasa and munondo trees, which have rough, fire-resistant bark, live on the Highveld amidst a sea of grasses. The grass is cut and used as thatching material for roofs. In the western part of Zimbabwe, the most common tree is the mopane. Caterpillars that live on mopane trees are a favorite fried snack. The drought-resistant, long-living baobab tree is found in the Lowveld, along with low, thorny scrub. Elephants gouge baobab tree trunks to eat. Other animals—and some humans—hollow out the trunks to live inside them. The Eastern Highlands are covered with wattle, eucalyptus, and pine forests, as well as with ferns and many wild flowers, including the protea. The flame lily is the national flower. The area immediately around Victoria Falls is a rain forest created by the constant water spray from the falls.

A **baobab tree** has a distinctive shape. It can grow up to 60 feet (18 m) tall and 30 to 50 feet (9 to 15 m) wide. The baobab's big trunk holds a lot of water, an important trait in a dry land.

Ecology and Wildlife Conservation

Zimbabwe's ecology is threatened by the cities and farms that grew throughout the twentieth century, destroying natural habitats. In the twenty-first century, social and political changes have led to further threats, including high unemployment. Many jobless urban people have moved back to the land to try to make a living. Overpopulation, overgrazing, the cutting of trees for fuel and the resulting soil erosion all lead to desertification—the process of fertile land becoming desert. Drought has magnified the effects.

Millions of acres of land are set aside for wildlife reserves, but the government has been reluctant or unable to supply the resources needed to run them. The parks offer wildlife human-made watering holes, which are expensive to maintain. Wildlife poaching (illegal hunting) is a challenge to manage as well. Rhinoceroses have been poached almost to extinction for their horns. Zimbabwe's shoot-to-kill policy toward poachers is controversial since many people poach animals with snares simply to feed their families.

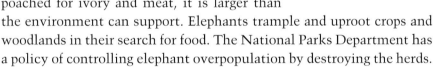

A watchful park ranger

Although the elephant population is still poached for ivory and meat, it is larger than the environment can support. Elephants trample and uproot crops and woodlands in their search for food. The National Parks Department has a policy of controlling elephant overpopulation by destroying the herds.

Safari tourism was once a profitable industry in Zimbabwe. Money from tourism helped to fund animal conservation programs. Some tourists paid many thousands of U.S. dollars for controlled permits to hunt large game animals. Independently owned game farms and safari camps were able to breed and conserve endangered species. Political and economic problems in the twenty-first century, however, have caused the tourist industry to collapse, and this source of income has disappeared. The commercial game farms, which previously were white-owned, have been seized by government-sponsored groups, and approximately 80 percent of the animals on them have been killed.

Climate

Since Zimbabwe lies in the tropics (the surface of the earth lying near the equator), it might be expected to be a land of tropical heat. Because of its altitude, however, Zimbabwe has one of the most moderate climates in the world. The country's inland location also helps to prevent excessive humidity. Located in the Southern Hemisphere, Zimbabwe has seasons that are the reverse of those in North America. Temperatures in the Highveld average 72°F (22°C) in October and dip to averages of 55°F (13°C) in July. The Lowveld is hotter, averaging 86°F (30°C) in October and 68°F (20°C) in July. Sunny winter days are followed by freezing cold winter nights throughout the country.

Zimbabwe has a rainy and a dry season. The rains come during November through March, bringing a freshened atmosphere and lush vegetation to all areas. As the rainless months progress, these effects lessen gradually until the countryside becomes brown and dry. If the rains come too late, drought can cause serious damage to crops. The economy, which is largely agricultural, can be seriously affected at such times, and life for rural people can be very difficult. Rainfall is extremely variable, with some regions never getting enough rain for agriculture. The Eastern Highlands averages 55 inches (140 centimeters) per year, the Highveld receives 31 inches (80 cm), and the Limpopo Valley in the Lowveld, only 16 inches (40 cm).

> Spectacular clouds and thunderstorms make for dramatic summer weather in Zimbabwe, and death by lightning is more common here than most places.

◉ Cities

HARARE, the capital of Zimbabwe, has many of the features of modern, international urban centers, including skyscrapers and well-kept parks. It is located in the region called Mashonaland, where most Shona live. The name Harare is derived from Ne-Hrawa, the chief of the original Shona inhabitants. Harare is often called the City of Flowering Trees because of its abundance of blossoms, including purple-hued jacaranda, red royal poinciana, and pastel bauhinia trees.

The capital has grown from flat plains to a sophisticated city of approximately 2 million people. On September 12, 1890, the first white settlers of the British South Africa Company (BSAC) camped on an open plain at the end of their long journey from Bechuanaland (modern-day Botswana). White settlers and merchants took the land and in 1897 declared it a municipality named Salisbury in honor of Robert Gascoyne-Cecil (Lord Salisbury), then prime minister of Great Britain. Its name was changed to Harare when Zimbabwe achieved independence in 1980. Since colonial days, the city has served as the nation's administrative hub. It also functions as the main distribution point of the area's agricultural goods and mining products. The country's tobacco crop is auctioned off in Harare between April and October each year.

Zimbabwe's capital city, Harare, was designed to have broad streets.

BULAWAYO was built on the site of the village founded by Lobengula, the leader of the Ndebele people, in 1881. The village was burned in 1894 as the chief fled from the BSAC forces, who assumed control over the region. The area around Bulawayo is called Matabeleland and is inhabited mostly by Ndebele people. Bulawayo is Zimbabwe's second largest city. Its 1 million inhabitants live at an elevation of 4,450 feet (1,356 m) above sea level. Like Harare, Bulawayo has a pleasant climate. As the center of Zimbabwe's railway system, Bulawayo became one of the most important cities in southern Africa for industry and commerce. The area around Bulawayo features the granite landscape of Matopos National Park, where rock paintings and rhinoceroses can be seen.

CHITUNGWIZA is a satellite town of Harare that arose because of the huge influx of people into Harare after independence. Sometimes it is counted as part of Harare, but it is a city in its own right with a population close to 1 million, a large number of whom live in poverty.

MUTARE (formerly Umtali), with a population of 200,000, is situated in a valley of the scenic Vumba Mountains. The city is the country's eastern gateway because it lies in the middle of the 200-mile (322-km) long Eastern Highlands, which form much of Zimbabwe's border with Mozambique. Land mines from civil wars in the two countries still make the border dangerous. Situated on the Harare-Beira Railway line, Mutare is a central point for the shipment of locally produced citrus fruits, tea, tobacco, and timber.

HISTORY AND GOVERNMENT

Zimbabwe has been inhabited since prehistoric times. Anthropologists believe that ancestors of modern humans lived on the grasslands of southern Africa about three million years ago. About 750,000 years ago, early species of humans were hunting large animals, including elephants, with crude stone tools. Archaeologists have found evidence of *Homo sapiens* (modern human beings) living in the area of Zimbabwe perhaps as many as 100,000 years ago. Rock paintings and well-made tools provide evidence of these people.

◗ Early Inhabitants

By 20,000 years ago, groups of organized hunters and gatherers inhabited the territory of present-day Zimbabwe. They used fire and made sophisticated tools of wood, stone, and animal parts. Their natural-pigment paintings on rocks and in caves portray animals and hunting and dancing scenes. These groups were related to the Khoisan peoples. About one thousand years ago, their descendants, the San (formerly known as

Bushmen), came into contact with newcomers to the area, the Shona-speaking people. The Shona people, who practiced mixed farming (crops and livestock), entered the region probably to escape the spreading deserts of North Africa. The Shona gradually conquered and intermarried with the San, while some of the San were pushed into the dry regions of modern-day Botswana, Namibia, and South Africa. The Shona grew grains and raised livestock, especially cattle, which were a source of milk, leather, wealth, and social status. Settled groups developed skills for iron working, textile weaving, pottery making, and the mining and trading of precious metals, especially gold.

Trade and Great Zimbabwe

Southern Africans began trading with Arab merchants in the A.D. 900s. Swahili (African coastal people) traders traveled between inland sites and the commercial centers on Africa's Indian Ocean coast. This trade led to the rise of a powerful Shona Empire in Zimbabwe. The Shona dynasties

GREAT ZIMBABWE

The ruins of the wealthy, powerful stone city—Great Zimbabwe—are one of the most important archaeological sites in Africa. The name Zimbabwe is derived from Shona *dzimba dza mabwe*, meaning "great stone houses." Located in southeastern Zimbabwe near Masvingo, Great Zimbabwe was built by Shona-speaking peoples starting about 1000 A.D. This city of religious and royal buildings is estimated to have once served a population of between ten thousand and twenty thousand people. Its most striking feature was a hilltop citadel *(above)*, or a shrine and a fortress protecting this political, economic, and cultural center. By the 1400s, Great Zimbabwe had started to decline, probably due to overpopulation and depletion of resources. People slowly moved away to more fertile areas, and other dynasties arose.

(families of rulers) traded ivory, rhinoceros horn, cloth, gold, and other valuable items for a wide variety of goods. Ruins of stone settlements from this phase of Zimbabwe's history can be found throughout the country. Persian, Indian, and Chinese articles, including glass beads and fabrics, have been excavated at these sites, demonstrating how widespread trading networks were.

◉ The Shona State and the Portuguese

During the 1400s, most of modern-day Zimbabwe was ruled by Shona hereditary kings known as Monomotapa (from Mwene, meaning "king" and Mutapa, meaning "conqueror"). From their walled cities in the northeast, these monarchs traded locally mined metals with merchants who arrived via the Indian Ocean.

Merchants and adventurers from Portugal arrived on the Indian Ocean coast in the early sixteenth century. By 1528 the Portuguese were trading in the interior of southern Africa, following the Zambezi River inland. They started colonies there in 1541, the first Europeans to do so. They introduced their Christian religion, which was not accepted by many, as well as corn, tobacco, and citrus fruits from the Americas, which were widely accepted. The Portuguese dealt in slaves too, but slavery did not become a large part of Zimbabwean trade or culture.

The Monomotapa kingdom in the north remained powerful until it was challenged by the Rozvi, a southwestern group. The Rozvi established the Changamire Empire in the late 1600s. They conquered the northern Shona peoples and drove the Portuguese out of the territory of modern-day Zimbabwe. The Portuguese retained their colonies in Portuguese East Africa (modern-day Mozambique).

New world trade routes led to the decline of the Indian Ocean trade in the early nineteenth century. As a result, the Changamire Empire weakened. Gradually, the unity of the kingdom diminished, causing the various Shona peoples to separate into many small groups.

Also in the early decades of the 1800s, the Shona began to come into contact with groups fleeing the *mfecane* (troubles) in the area that in modern times is South Africa. The mfecane aided the rise of Shaka, the ruler of the Zulu people. A powerful and militarily skilled monarch, Shaka—with the aid of his warriors—established a vast empire. Mzilikazi, one of Shaka's war leaders, left the king's domain, taking with him a large following. Shaka pursued, and Mzilikazi fled north. Harassed by both Shaka's forces and white settlers, Mzilikazi and his people finally established themselves near the modern-day city of Bulawayo in 1839. There he established his kingdom, later called Matabeleland. These newcomers to the area came to be called Ndebele, from a local word meaning "strangers."

◉ Missionaries and Colonization

Christian missionaries (people who work to spread their religion) were part of a revived European interest in establishing new colonies in areas of southern Africa as yet untouched by white people. Missionaries befriended Mzilikazi, and he gave his permission for a mission school to be started in 1859. The work of the missionaries who wanted to convert the native people to Christianity was paired with exploration by Europeans, who wanted to open the area to trade. They were searching for valuable trade goods, including ostrich feathers, animal skins, and ivory.

When Mzilikazi died in 1868, he was succeeded by his son Lobengula. At this time, many European powers were scrambling to claim land in Africa. Cecil Rhodes, a rich, enterprising, and forceful British financier, envisioned the whole of southern Africa as a huge British colony. He didn't want the non-British white settlers of South Africa or Mozambique to gain control of the area.

Cecil Rhodes was very successful. He was able to buy out the large diamond mining companies in southern Africa by writing a personal check written for the huge total (in British pounds) of "Five million, Three Hundred and Thirty-Eight Thousand, Six Hundred and Fifty-Eight Pounds-Only."

More than any other individual, Cecil Rhodes was responsible for the British colonization of Zimbabwe. (Rhodesia—which included present-day Zimbabwe and Zambia—was named after Rhodes.) He dominated the politics of southern Africa and created a large personal financial empire. He considered the British "the best people in the world" and wanted all of Africa to be part of the British Empire.

Rhodes sought from Lobengula to monopolize (completely control) all mining rights in the Ndebele kingdom. In exchange, Lobengula was to receive one hundred British pounds each month, one thousand modern guns, and a gunboat. But Rhodes tricked Lobengula, who could not read, and the written agreement the king actually signed granted far more to the British than he had consented to verbally. Rhodes started his own company, the British South Africa Company (BSAC) and soon came with a force of hired soldiers to take over the land.

Rhodes obtained a twenty-five-year royal charter (a written contract granting rights) in October 1889 from Queen Victoria of Great Britain to rule the lands of the Shona (called Mashonaland) and the Ndebele (Matabeleland). He hired troops to occupy the Shona territories in 1890 under the BSAC. On September 12, 1890, these occupying forces built a fort near some Shona villages. The two hundred British settlers—frequently termed the Pioneer Column—called their new post Salisbury. Without seeking permission from the local black leaders, Rhodes granted fertile farmland and mining claims to his troops. Within two years, white settlers numbered three thousand.

African Resistance

The Shona and the Ndebele, at first, had accepted the white settlers as *vaeni* (friendly strangers) with whom they could trade cattle and goods. The Africans thought that the vaeni would stay for only a short time. The whites established settlements throughout the Shona lands, however, and pushed Africans off the fertile lands and onto poor-quality reserves. The Shona, who had not made an agreement with the British, blamed Lobengula, who had.

In July 1893, one of the regiments under Lobengula's command attacked Shona villagers because they had taken some cattle from the Ndebele. This event gave the British an excuse to go to war against Lobengula.

With most of his soldiers fighting the Shona, Lobengula's remaining warriors were no match for the better-armed British forces. Lobengula fled north and died of fever in 1894. The British divided his lands among themselves, and the Africans living there were required to pay rent.

Two years later, the Ndebele and the Shona united against their common enemy and revolted against the white settlers. Eventually, the settlers subdued the Shona and the Ndebele with their superior weapons. African deaths numbered 8,000, while 372 white settlers were killed. The first war of liberation, called the First Chimurenga, was over.

Lobengula once told a missionary how a chameleon catches a fly. "The chameleon gets behind the fly, remains motionless for some time, then he advances very slowly and gently, first putting forward one leg and then another. At last, when well within reach, he darts his tongue and the fly disappears. England is the chameleon and I am that fly."

Self-Government and Black Opposition

When the first period of rule by the BSAC expired in 1914, the British government and the company officers (Rhodes had died in 1902) agreed that the charter should be extended. In 1922 white voters had to choose between self-government or incorporation into South Africa. (Blacks were effectively barred from voting by economic and literacy requirements they could not meet.) The white voters chose self-government, and on September 12, 1923, the colony of Southern Rhodesia was formally annexed (joined) to the British Crown. The country became a self-governing colony within the British Empire.

The white minority government of Southern Rhodesia passed laws that segregated blacks and denied them civil rights. Blacks were deprived of their ancestral lands. They did not have education, housing, or wages equal to whites. Because of this discrimination, Shona and Ndebele leaders cooperated to form the African National Congress (ANC) of Southern Rhodesia in 1932. They tried to work to reduce discrimination against blacks through legal means. The voters in Rhodesia, however, were not willing to grant blacks more political participation.

After World War II (1939–1945), more European settlers came to Rhodesia, especially war veterans leaving economically depressed postwar Europe. The Rhodesian government made it easy for new immigrants looking for fresh opportunities to establish large farms. More black Rhodesians were forced off their lands.

Federation and New Political Groups

In 1953 Southern Rhodesia entered into a federation (limited political union) with Northern Rhodesia (modern Zambia) and Nyasaland (modern Malawi) called the Central African Federation. The association was meant to strengthen the countries politically and economically. Black Africans in all three territories, however, were strongly opposed to this federation, because it was ruled by the white minority population.

In 1960 British prime minister Harold Macmillan observed that "winds of change" were blowing, as many of Britain's African colonies were demanding independence. Most white Rhodesians strongly resisted these changes. The ANC was banned, but leaders among the black population organized new political groups. In 1961 the Zimbabwe African People's Union (ZAPU) was founded by Joshua Nkomo, an Ndebele, and Robert Mugabe, a Shona. The purpose of their organization was to work for democratic rule. The colonial government outlawed ZAPU in September 1962. Disagreements arose between Nkomo and Mugabe. Mugabe left ZAPU and helped form a separate organization, the Zimbabwe African National Union (ZANU) to fight minority rule.

For ten years, black Africans of the Central African Federation demanded the right to separate. In April 1963, the British government finally announced that any of the territories had the right to leave the federation. The federation was dissolved on December 31, 1963. Zambia and Malawi became independent nations in 1964.

Unilateral Declaration of Independence (UDI) and Sanctions

Many white Rhodesians objected to what they saw as the British government's appeasement of black Africans. Whites were unwilling to give up their rights to the best lands, jobs, privilege, and political power. The Rhodesian Front (RF) was formed to uphold white rule and to push for full independence from Great Britain. Great Britain refused to grant independence unless Southern Rhodesia moved toward black majority rule.

The RF appointed Ian Smith to be prime minister in 1964. He ruled over 200,000 whites and 4 million blacks. Smith said, "I don't believe in black majority rule in Rhodesia, not in a thousand years." On November

In 1965 a **headline about the Unilateral Declaration of Independence (UDI)** in the *Rhodesian Herald* sold a lot of papers in Rhodesia. A photo of prime minister Ian Smith appears on the front page too.

11, 1965, Smith made a Unilateral Declaration of Independence (UDI) from Great Britain. The UDI gave the country, renamed Rhodesia, complete authority over its own affairs. Great Britain declared the action illegal and stopped all trade with Rhodesia.

Soon after, other countries also placed economic pressure on Rhodesia to end minority rule. The United Nations (an international organization for handling global disputes) and countries in Africa and the western world imposed sanctions against the new republic, forbidding any trade or diplomatic relations with Rhodesia.

Civil War

After the UDI, the African nationalist opposition began a war of liberation, called the Second Chimurenga, to overthrow Smith's government. In 1966 the exiled ZANU began sending trained guerrilla fighters back into Rhodesia from Zambia to conduct hit-and-run raids on white targets. In July 1967, Nkomo's ZAPU forces first fought Rhodesian government troops, near Hwange.

On March 2, 1970, Rhodesia officially became a republic with a new constitution designed to guarantee continued white rule. Great Britain, the United Nations, and the black majority in Rhodesia did not recognize the event.

By 1972 a full-scale civil war was in progress in Rhodesia. Many young people, men and women, joined ZANU and ZAPU. Small groups learned how to survive and fight as free roaming bands all over the country. The black majority called these guerrillas freedom fighters while the white regime called them terrorists. Their actions against government troops, civilians, and white-owned farms and businesses caused destruction, economic hardship, casualties, and low white morale. As the fighting continued, the guerrillas gained support from the majority of the black population. Guerrillas also held teaching sessions in rural areas and explained the war's goals of majority rule and the return of ancestral lands. Rural people supported the guerrillas with food, clothing, and information. Smith's government forced rural Zimbabweans into isolated camps to prevent the local populations from supporting the rebels. This action increased resistance to the established government.

By late 1975—despite harsh reprisals, torture of civilians, and military-imposed law throughout the country—the Zimbabwean guerrillas were wearing down the Rhodesian government forces and the white population. Though neither side was officially winning the war, economic hardship from international sanctions combined with years of guerrilla attacks on white targets weakened the white regime.

Zimbabwean Independence

On March 3, 1978, in a last attempt to retain minority power over crumbling Rhodesian affairs, Ian Smith convinced Abel Muzorewa, a Methodist bishop, and some other black leaders to join in a coalition (multi-party) government. This government—rejected by all of the guerrilla leaders—lasted about a year. After the breakdown of the coalition, Great Britain proposed meetings in London to consider how to resolve the conflict.

From September 10 to December 21, 1979, the Patriotic Front (PF)—led jointly by Robert Mugabe and Joshua Nkomo with delegates from both ZANU and ZAPU—met at Lancaster House in London with

Bishop Muzorewa, Smith, and others in a constitutional conference. The delegates ironed out a cease-fire, wrote a new constitution, and made arrangements for governing the country in the interim period between the end of the civil war and the establishment of the republic of Zimbabwe. Estimates indicate that thirty thousand Zimbabweans—mostly guerrilla fighters—had died in the conflict.

From December 1979 to April 17, 1980, the country was again ruled as the British colony of Southern Rhodesia (called Zimbabwe-Rhodesia). International sanctions were lifted. On April 18, 1980, the former colony began its history as an independent country officially named the Republic of Zimbabwe with majority rule.

The Postindependence Era

After the establishment of the Republic of Zimbabwe, the new government—with war hero Robert Mugabe overwhelmingly elected as prime minister—aimed to heal the divisions created by the civil war. Ian Smith, for example, retained his parliamentary seat and freely debated his views in the legislature. In addition, Joshua Nkomo—Mugabe's longtime rival—became a member of the new cabinet. Hopes were high that this new government could achieve racial, economic, and social well-being.

Immediately after independence, the situation in Zimbabwe looked optimistic. Educational and rural health facilities expanded rapidly. Black Zimbabweans entered the civil service (the administrative sector of government) in large numbers. People who had left or been exiled, both black and white, returned to help the country.

The biggest challenge the Mugabe government faced upon independence was the issue of land reform. The most productive agricultural land had been owned for generations by whites. Black peasants, poor people, workers, and women had fought a long, bitter war to gain land. Mugabe had promised to resettle blacks on white-owned land

Bob Marley and the Wailers, the Jamaican reggae music superstar and his band, perform Marley's song "Zimbabwe" during the Zimbabwe Independence Celebration at the Great Zimbabwe ruins on April 18, 1980. He had written the song—after visiting Rhodesia in 1978—in solidarity with the Zimbabweans' struggle for self-rule in their nation.

after the war. The farmers were to be paid market price for their land, with the economic assistance of Great Britain. It was largely agreed that land needed to be redistributed, but the large, white-owned commercial farms were the country's main source of foreign income. The sale of tobacco, for instance, brought in large amounts of cash from international buyers. Few blacks, who had not received equal education under white rule, had the expertise to run sophisticated, agricultural businesses. Half the white population of Zimbabwe left after independence, but most white farmers who stayed kept their land. Little of the land that was bought by the government was distributed to landless people, including the many black workers employed on the farms. Most of it went to Mugabe's political supporters and members of the ruling elite.

The process of political cooperation did not last long. Smith's RF split into factions. Violent clashes between armed war veterans of the different groups left hundreds dead. Nkomo was dismissed from the cabinet in 1982 after he was accused of supporting antigovernment rebels in Matabeleland, where most Ndebele lived. Mugabe aimed to remove his main rival, ZAPU, and create a one-party state where he would have no political opposition.

In the early 1980s, fighting erupted between the Ndebele people—a minority group that supported ZAPU,

MUGABE SPEAKS

"If yesterday I fought you as an enemy, today you have become a friend and an ally with the same national interest, loyalty, rights and duties as myself.... The wrongs of the past must now stand forgiven and forgotten. If ever we look to the past, let us do so for the lesson the past has taught us, namely that oppression and racism are inequalities that must never find scope in our political and social system. It could never be a correct justification that because whites oppressed us yesterday when they had power, the blacks must oppress them today because they have power. An evil remains an evil whether practiced by white against black or black against white."

—Robert Mugabe (right), in a speech about the achievement of national independence in 1980

Nkomo's opposition party—and the majority Shona, who backed Mugabe's ZANU-PF. The redistribution of land was a source of discontent. Rivalries flared into violent repression in Matabeleland. The government had kept in place Ian Smith's 1965 state of emergency, which gave the government broad police powers, including the right to arrest people without charging them with a crime. Mugabe's government created the Fifth Brigade, a special army brigade made up mostly of Shona and trained by North Korean advisers. The Fifth Brigade carried out a brutal *gukurahundi,* or wiping away, that is thought to have killed twenty-five thousand Ndebele and brutalized many more.

Violence overshadowed the 1985 elections. Voters gave Mugabe's ZANU-PF party a majority of seats, and he won another term as prime minister.

In 1985 Nkomo began talks with Mugabe to end the division between their two groups. The outcome of their discussions was a 1987 agreement to merge Nkomo's ZAPU party with the dominant ZANU-PF party. This move effectively made Zimbabwe a one-party state under Mugabe's rule.

Under the 1987 agreement, Mugabe broadened his powers. He became Zimbabwe's executive president—a new position that combines the posts of prime minister and president. He also was named president and first secretary of ZANU-PF. In this way, he was able to gain great personal power. Through a network of patronage (using personal power to give jobs or favors in exchange for political advantages), he established control of the media; police and security forces; the large state-controlled sector of the economy; civil service; and eventually, the courts. Mugabe's autocratic rule led to an increasingly undemocratic government.

Election campaigning in 1990 was characterized by suppression of opposition. Many university students supported Edgar Tekere's opposition party Zimbabwe Unity Movement (ZUM). When students tried to demonstrate against government corruption, police forcibly prevented them and arrested student leaders. Morgan Tsvangirai, leader of the Zimbabwe Congress of Trade Unions, said the events were "a clear manifestation of rising state repression." He was arrested too. Mugabe won his second term with 80 percent of the votes. Only 54 percent of those eligible voted, however. The 1965 state of emergency was finally lifted, but the one-party government maintained broad powers.

In 1996 Mugabe won a third term as president. Legislative elections had confirmed the overwhelming majority of the ZANU-PF party, which held 148 of the 150 seats in the House of Assembly. But opposition groups accused the government of manipulating the vote and boycotted the elections. Dissidents (people who disagree with a political system) in Zimbabwe and exiled in neighboring Mozambique increasingly protested Mugabe's rule.

BLOOD DIAMONDS

Although Zimbabwe produces few diamonds, it is involved in illegal diamond trading through the Democratic Republic of Congo. Mugabe sent troops in 1998 to the war-torn Congo to support the government of Laurent Kabila, who traded mineral rights for Zimbabwean troops. Kabila was assassinated in 2001. The cost in money and lives made the war unpopular in Zimbabwe, but some Zimbabweans made a lot of money dealing what are called "blood" or "conflict" diamonds—gems mined in war zones.

In 1998 Zimbabwean troops entered the Democratic Republic of Congo. They supported President Laurent Kabila in a civil war against Rwanda- and Uganda-backed rebels. Wealth from the Congo's diamond and gold mines and timber was given to some Zimbabwean government officials in exchange for this support. Involvement in the foreign war was extremely unpopular in Zimbabwe, even among some military leaders, as it cost vast sums of money. As Zimbabwean casualties grew and the economy slumped, Mugabe's popular support eroded. Riots and strikes protested government mismanagement of the economy and the resulting unemployment and high prices of basic goods, food, and fuel.

⊙ Land Invasions

In 2000 the white population, which composed 1 percent of the total population, still owned much of the nation's best farmland. That year Mugabe responded to pressures from war veterans to live up to his promise of land redistribution. The war veterans were increasingly unhappy with the government they had fought to install. High unemployment and inflation plagued the country.

Mugabe was also facing unprecedented political opposition from a new political party, the Movement for Democratic Change (MDC), and he needed to strengthen his support. He announced plans for a fast-track campaign for seizure of white-owned farms. He declared that since much of the land had originally been seized from black Africans, the current owners were not to be paid. Under the terms of Zimbabwe's constitution, this was illegal, but Mugabe declared that even the farms bought by whites after 1980 with government approval could be seized without payment. Loosely organized groups of war veterans and others occupied farms by force. The occupations soon turned into invasions as white farm families were evicted, and both

Because of high inflation, the largest denomination of Zimbabwe currency, in Zimbabwean dollars (ZWD), a 1,000 note, cannot buy one loaf of bread.

whites and blacks were beaten or even killed. Farms were burned and looted, animals were slaughtered, and thousands of black farmworkers lost their livelihoods.

Within months, only a few hundred of the four thousand white Zimbabwean farmers remained on their land. Squatters (illegal settlers) flooded onto the land in large numbers but lacked seeds, equipment, money, and farming know-how. Drought made the circumstances worse. Once rich farmland was reduced to farm plots that could barely support the people living on them. Within four years, Zimbabwe, a country that once exported food, had become dependent on foreign food aid to avoid famine.

Movement for Democratic Change Followed by Corrupt Elections

Troops were withdrawn from the Congo in 2002 at the end of the war. But discontent in Zimbabwe grew as conditions throughout the country worsened. By 2002 the rate of AIDS was 33 percent, unemployment was at 70 percent, inflation was at 500 percent, and the United Nations warned that millions of Zimbabweans faced starvation. Human rights monitors reported an increase in human rights abuses. To prevent criticism and to maintain power, Mugabe's government moved to take control of the Supreme Court, banned television debates, and tried to silence journalists. Political intimidation increased.

In the 2002 presidential elections, the Movement for Democratic Change presented a challenge to Mugabe and his one-party rule. Morgan

During a **drought** watering holes such as this one near Sanyatwe, Zimbabwe, may go dry. Livestock may have to travel great distances for water.

Tsvangirai, a former union leader, is the head of the MDC. He has mobilized a wide range of people, including young people, urban workers, and white farmers, who oppose Mugabe's hold on the country. In the twelve months before the 2002 presidential elections, specially trained government forces used violence, intimidation, arrest, torture, and murder to create a climate of fear for those who might vote against Mugabe and ZANU-PF. More than thirty people who supported the opposition were killed in the two months before the election.

In an election that international observers widely reported as corrupt, Mugabe won with 56 percent of the vote. Leaders of the Commonwealth of Nations (an organization of fifty-four countries, mostly former British territories), which is committed to democratic values and freedoms, suspended Zimbabwe from the organization. Zimbabwe later resigned from the organization. The International Monetary Fund (IMF) and the World Bank (United Nations agencies that lend money and offer economic development advice to countries) also expelled Zimbabwe for the government's economic mismanagement.

A 2003 general strike was organized by opposition groups to protest the country's conditions and to call for Mugabe's early retirement. It was met with arrests and beatings of hundreds of people. Despite government suppression, the MDC continued its opposition. The 2005 parliamentary elections will be followed by the next presidential election in 2008.

Visit www.vgsbooks.com for links to websites with more information about the history of Zimbabwe.

Governmental Structure

The 1987 agreement between Mugabe and Nkomo brought about a major change in the structure of Zimbabwe's government. Formerly a parliamentary democracy—with a head of government (the prime minister) and a head of state (the president)—Zimbabwe combines the jobs of prime minister and president into the office of executive president.

The executive president is elected to a six-year term by a vote in the legislature. These votes are determined by a popular vote. The executive president names vice presidents, cabinet ministers, and members of the judicial branch. The executive president can also veto legislation passed by the parliament.

Parliament is made up of a one-house legislature known as the House of Assembly. Members of the House of Assembly are elected to five-year terms. Of the 150 legislators, 120 are elected by a popular vote, 10 hold seats as tribal chiefs, 12 are appointed by the Zimbabwean president, and

8 hold seats as provincial governors. A two-thirds majority in the House of Assembly is necessary to make changes to the constitution. The constitution guarantees majority rule and protects minority rights. A declaration of rights guarantees fundamental rights and freedoms of all Zimbabwean citizens.

Bills passed by the House of Assembly are presented to the executive president. If the executive president accepts the bill, it becomes a law that governs the country. A presidential veto of a piece of legislation can be overridden if two-thirds of the members of the legislature vote to support the bill.

The president appoints the country's justices. A chief justice and at least two other justices preside over the Zimbabwean Supreme Court. The Supreme Court enforces the Declaration of Rights and serves as the final court of appeal. The chief justice also heads the High Court, which holds authority over all of the country's trials. Regional and magistrate courts hear criminal cases. Local courts decide civil and minor criminal cases.

For administrative purposes, Zimbabwe is divided into eight provinces. A governor, whom the executive president appoints, administers each province with the help of local ministries.

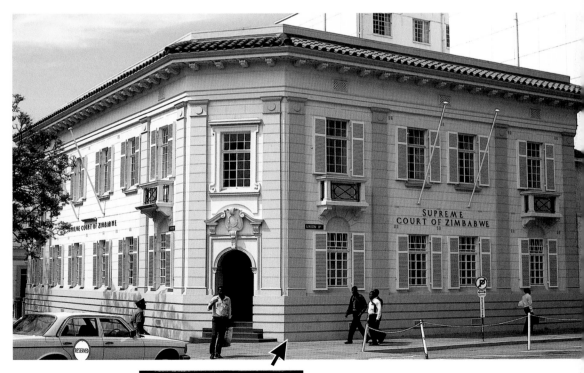

In October 2004, **Zimbabwe's Supreme Court,** which meets in this building in Harare, cleared opposition leader Morgan Tsvangirai of the false charge of plotting to assassinate President Mugabe before the 2002 elections.

THE PEOPLE

In the first years of Zimbabwe's independence, hopes were high that the country would be able to break with the inequalities of the past. Initially, great improvements were made in living conditions. In the twenty-first century, however, many of Zimbabwe's 12.7 million people face struggles that threaten the entire fabric of society. Like most countries in southern Africa, Zimbabwe has been hard hit by HIV/AIDS. The government is committed to fighting the disease, but health and education services have deteriorated because of the nation's economic difficulties. The prevalence (rate of infection) of HIV/AIDS among adults aged 15 to 49 years old is 33 percent. The pandemic (disease outbreak affecting an exceptionally high proportion of people) has resulted in lower life expectancy, higher infant death rates, and lower population growth rates. Children under the age of 14 make up 40 percent of the population.

Worsening the situation is the food shortage that has ravaged the country since 2000. The harvest of corn, the country's dietary staple,

has fallen by one-half because of drought and the destruction of large-scale agriculture. Because of high unemployment, people often don't have money for food even when food is available. The United Nations and other relief agencies have stated that more than 7 million Zimbabweans have no ready access to a minimum of daily food and need foreign food donations to survive. Chronic hunger invites a host of diseases that further weaken the population.

Language

Several languages are spoken in Zimbabwe. English, the official language, is the language of government, law, and business. It is spoken by the white population and understood—if not always used—by more than half of the black citizens, especially by urban dwellers. Many Zimbabwean authors write in English. Most Zimbabweans speak one of several Bantu languages. Bantu, which means "people," is a family of Niger-Congo languages spoken in central and southern Africa. The

SHONA WAS OUR LANGUAGE

" 'They don't understand Shona very well anymore,' her mother explained. 'They have been speaking nothing but English for so long that most of their Shona has gone.'

"What Maiguru said was bewildering, bewildering and offending. I had not expected my cousins to have changed, certainly not so radically, simply because they had been away for a while. Besides, Shona was our language. What did people mean when they forgot it? Standing there, trying to digest these thoughts, I remembered speaking to my cousins freely and fluently before they went away, eating wild fruits with them, making clay pots and swimming in the Nyamarira. Now they had turned into strangers. I stopped being offended and was sad instead."

—Tsitsi Dangarembga, *Nervous Conditions*, 1988

two most common ones in Zimbabwe are Shona or Ndebele. Shona is a mix of several Bantu languages. The Shona people all speak dialects of the same language. The Ndebele language derives from a Zulu group of languages. It has a series of clicking noises. Each click comes in four different varieties, which are very difficult for nonnative speakers to pronounce.

Chilapalapa is a pidgin language (a simplified language for use between people who speak different tongues). It is a crude mix of English, Afrikaans, and Bantu languages and was invented in the underground mines so that white bosses could communicate with their African workers who spoke different languages. While Ndebele and Shona stress formal, polite speech, Chilapalapa does not.

◉ Ethnic Composition

Most of Zimbabwe's 12.7 million people are either Shona or Ndebele. These groups are not ethnically different, but rather speak different languages. The Shona people make up about 82 percent of the population. Most of the country's leaders, including President Mugabe, are Shona. The Ndebele represent about 14 percent of the population and are centered in Matabeleland, the area around Bulawayo.

Relations between these two main groups have not always been smooth. The Ndebele who moved north from South Africa were warriorlike people. They invaded Shona territory, taxed the Shona, and pushed them eastward. This history has affected relations between the two groups ever since. The primarily Shona government sent the Fifth Brigade into Matabeleland in the early

1980s, and they carried out a campaign of terror. Tensions between the two groups remain.

Several other smaller, black African groups, including the Shangaan, Tonga, Venda, and Sotho peoples, make up about 2 percent of the population. Only an estimated 500 San live in Zimbabwe. People of mixed and Asian heritage constitute 1 percent of the population. Whites—who fled the country in large numbers just after independence and again after the land occupations starting in 2000—make up less than 1 percent. More than 75 percent of the whites, who are primarily of British origin, are urban dwellers. Roughly the same percentage of blacks live in rural areas.

Village and Family Life

Though Zimbabwean society has been greatly affected by colonization, wars of independence, and contemporary hardships, the culture retains its traditional roots, especially in rural areas. Life in villages is community based. Religion is interwoven through every aspect of social life and custom. Many believe that the community includes the spiritual presence of ancestors. These spirits are believed to communicate through a living person called a medium, who is consulted for important decisions, including the appointment of a village chief. A council of men helps the chief make decisions for the group based on customary law.

The family is patrilineal, or traces descent through the male line. The family unit is very tight and strong, especially in rural areas. Duties are determined by gender and age. Men do the heaviest work, and men and boys take care of the cattle. Women and girls tend to household work, which can be extremely labor intensive and

> "An anthropologist said, 'When I'm with the old people, I have to remind myself they live in a different landscape. Each rock, tree, path, hill, bird, animal, has a meaning. If an owl calls or you see a certain bird, that is a message from another dimension. A pebble set near a path is part of a pattern. You see a bit of rag tied to a bush—watch out! It's a bit of magic, most likely. Don't disturb! . . . When I'm with the old ones I sometimes get a glimpse of a landscape that existed everywhere in the world before modern man arrived on the scene.' "
>
> —Doris Lessing, white Zimbabwean author, *African Laughter*, 1992

Three **women in rural Zimbabwe,** including a woman carrying a child on her back *(center),* brace themselves to carry home enormous bundles of firewood.

include carrying water long distances, gathering firewood, and grinding corn by hand. Both sexes farm the land. Old age is respected, and children are expected to be obedient.

A man must pay a bride-price, called *lobola,* in cattle to the father of the woman he wishes to marry. Cattle traditionally were and remain the most important source of wealth and social standing, but in modern times, men may offer money as lobola. Men may marry as many women as they can support financially.

Traditionally, women had been considered minors in the eyes of the law and were under the guardianship of husbands and male relatives. Women were actively involved in the Second Chimurenga, sometimes as guerrilla fighters. After the war, women organized for equal social and legal rights. In 1982 women were declared to be legal adults. Village-based projects have brought women together in business ventures, such as sewing school uniforms or raising chickens, to supplement farming incomes. Projects also deal with issues such as reducing domestic violence, increasing literacy, and improving the legal status of women. Traditional structures have favored men over women, and many social and cultural obstacles to change remain.

Urban life is much more westernized than is rural life. In big cities, the roles of men and women have changed and are not as clearly defined. Migration to the cities and emigration to other countries in search of work has changed family patterns. AIDS and famine have also weakened the family unit as it is increasingly unable to bear the burden of caring for orphaned children in poverty.

Education

Traditional precolonial education taught children culture, history, religion, and life skills through spoken word, music, dance, and ritual. From the mid-1800s until about 1950, Christian missionaries provided most formal Western-style education. Some mission schools were integrated, teaching both black and white students. Before independence in 1980, only students of European background received free and compulsory government-provided education. Black children had to pay fees to attend segregated government schools. Literacy did not rise above 50 percent until after independence. Many adults, especially women, who had never received an education took advantage of adult literacy classes and other informal education. Zimbabwe's overall literacy rate has reached 90 percent, with women at 87 percent and men at 94 percent.

According to the constitution, the government provides free primary education to all children. By the mid-1990s, the country had built 4,500 primary and 1,500 secondary schools, often with the volunteer help of parents. A rapid school construction program allowed the number of secondary school students to increase by ten times between 1980 and 1995. The central government pays the salaries of the primary school teachers, but the schools themselves are owned and run by local councils, missions, business firms, and private individuals. In the twenty-first century, some school fees have been reintroduced. About 95 percent of all school-age children are enrolled in primary schools. Schoolbooks, materials, and qualified teachers remain in short supply. The Zimbabwean government hopes to be able to provide secondary schooling for all those who seek it, and 45 percent of the school-age population attend secondary school.

Students take an outdoor break from their studies at their **school in Madadzi,** Zimbabwe. To read more about the education and family lives of the people of Zimbabwe, stop by www.vgsbooks.com for links.

The University of Zimbabwe in Harare, founded in 1955, serves the higher educational needs of the country. Classes focus on agriculture, the arts, commerce, law, education, engineering, and medicine. The University of Science and Technology enrolls students at Bulawayo. Training for the mining industry is carried out by the Zimbabwe School of Mines. Zimbabwe also has two private universities, as well as teacher-training, agricultural, and technical colleges.

◎ Health Care and AIDS

During the first decade of independence, the government placed a strong emphasis on basic health care, and Zimbabwe's health care saw rapid improvements. Rural people worked to build health clinics, toilets, and wells for better health care, sanitation, and cleaner water. Courses on health education, care, and disease prevention were taught in villages. Health care was free for people with low incomes.

In the 1990s, the health sector started to decline under the burden of AIDS, economic strains, and food shortages. In 1999 Robert Mugabe's government levied an AIDS tax of 3 percent on every salary to pay for AIDS education, prevention, and treatment. Not all the money was used for these purposes. Decline in international donor assistance has negatively affected social and health services as well.

Neighbors work together at **Masvingo's community well** to pump clean water for their families.

In the twenty-first century, the health sector is severely affected by the general breakdown in the country. Low pay and a lack of basic medical equipment and medicines strain health services. Many health care workers have left for better conditions in other countries. Food shortages also strain the resources of hospitals. Widespread food and fuel shortages mean that some rural clinics have to function without reliable ambulance services or food for patients.

AIDS and AIDS-related illnesses are the most serious challenge facing the health system. Zimbabwe has one of the highest rates of infection in Africa, with an estimated one in three adults infected. Life expectancy in Zimbabwe was 62 years in the mid-1990s. Ten years later, life expectancy dropped to 39 years (40 years for men and 38 for women). Though the fertility rate is 3.7 children per woman, it is predicted that Zimbabwe will soon reach zero population growth. AIDS usually infects adults of working age, and AIDS illnesses and deaths of workers have led to an overall loss of productivity. The loss of teachers and government workers has serious implications for the running of the country.

The effect of AIDS is increased by social factors such as poverty and the status of women. Poverty is widespread, with 36 percent of the population living on less than $1 per day, and it leads to increases in malnutrition and general poor health. Malnutrition weakens the body's immune system and increases the speed and force of HIV/AIDS, as well as allowing other opportunistic diseases to strike. Medicines that help people live with AIDS have had good results, but they are too expensive for most Zimbabwean people and for the government health department.

Women generally have a lower social status and lack financial, social, and educational equality with men. They are more vulnerable

Nganga (traditional healers) are officially recognized figures in the health services of Zimbabwe. Some Nganga use herbs for their treatment of patients, while others rely on their knowledge of local customs and beliefs to cure or to prevent illness. Most nganga belong to the Zimbabwe National Traditional Healers Association (ZINATHA). Patients often consult a nganga and only approach modern medicine as a last resort. ZINATHA is working with the government's anti-AIDS campaign, using their position of respect in society to tackle this serious health issue.

to unsafe sexual practices. Polygamy (having multiple wives) increases the spread of the disease. Many men consider condoms unmanly and refuse to wear them. Only 53 percent of women use any method of birth control. The government has supported projects that promote family planning and the empowerment of rural and poor women. Women are actively involved in health care as midwives attending births and as trained village health workers.

A member of the **Gweru Women's AIDS Prevention Association (GWAPA)** in Gweru, Zimbabwe, knows the message on her tee shirt is urgent for the women and children of Zimbabwe. One of every three adults there is infected with the disease.

Children are also hard hit by AIDS and economic hardship. Approximately 40 percent of pregnant women are HIV positive (infected with HIV). They can pass the disease to their babies at birth. The infant mortality rate indicates that 66 out of 1,000 babies die before their first birthday. (The infant mortality rate in the United States is 6.7 per 1,000.) The mortality rate for children who are less than five years old is 108 per 1,000 children. More than 600,000 children have been orphaned by the death of their parents. Many of these children are forced to leave school to try to find work or to care for sick relatives. Traditionally families have always cared for their own, but some family systems have broken down completely. Children flood the country's limited orphanages or raise themselves and their younger siblings.

Studies have shown that strong leadership and commitment to education and prevention can halt or reverse the rapid spread of HIV/AIDS and save thousands of lives. Despite challenging times, the government has developed programs to combat AIDS. Zimbabwe's challenge is to continue to pay for and implement these plans.

CHILDREN ON THEIR OWN

"When I was six, I ran away to the streets of Harare. I learned to eat from garbage bins and to sleep on the verandas of shops. I guarded cars for money and sometimes begged. . . .

"Then [outreach workers of a children's home] invited me to come and stay. . . . To sleep inside a room, to have a bed, a blanket, and a chance to go to school is the best thing that has ever happened to me."

—Justice, a teenager at Mbuya Nehanda Training Center (MNTC), a farm residence for former street children

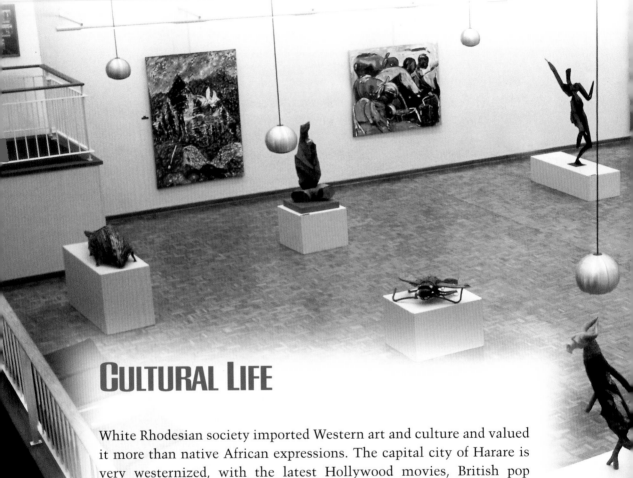

CULTURAL LIFE

White Rhodesian society imported Western art and culture and valued it more than native African expressions. The capital city of Harare is very westernized, with the latest Hollywood movies, British pop songs, and fast food. Under the veneer of Western culture, however, native Zimbabwean cultural activity continued to thrive, and independence brought a great burst of creative energy.

◉ Pieces of the Past

Some of the world's oldest art is found in southern Africa. Thousands of years ago, ancestors of the San created rock paintings that document their environment and hint at their religious beliefs. The paintings that survive are on the inside of cave walls or protected by rock overhangs. Giraffes, elephants, lions, rhinoceroses, antelopes, and the San's hunting techniques are realistically depicted in rich, earthy colors. The paints were made from powdered minerals mixed with animal fat, and they were applied with animal-hair brushes. The people believed

that their art had spiritual influence on their lives and the natural world. Depictions of trance dances and spiritual healing call upon the life force, known as *nxum*, which is still a part of San tradition. The San called on nxum to control weather, health, and other matters of life and death. The creative vision of these early people can best be seen in Zimbabwe at Matopos National Park near Bulawayo.

The architecture of the ancient city of Great Zimbabwe (CA. A.D. 1000 to 1500) attests to a long and sophisticated creative history. The city covers 1,779 acres (720 hectares), making it the largest of Zimbabwe's thirty-five thousand registered archaeological sites. Conical towers and long, curved walls made of complex stonework are the hallmarks of this ruined site. Soapstone carvings of birds found at the site are unlike sculpture found elsewhere, and the birds do not look like any local species. Each one is differently patterned. They are up to 14 inches (35 cm) high and many sit atop pillars that are 3 feet (1 m) tall. Some scholars think the birds may have been used in rituals to represent ancestors. The site is an important legacy of African culture. The very name of the country comes from it, and a Great Zimbabwe bird is represented on the country's flag.

◉ Shona Sculpture and Art in Life

Shona stone sculpture—perhaps the most significant development in Zimbabwean art or even in African art in the twentieth century— began in the workshop of Harare's National Gallery during the 1960s. Since then, these stone sculptures have achieved international recognition and are eagerly sought by art collectors. Working with locally quarried rock, the artists develop their own personal styles to create abstract figures based on animal and human forms. Sculptors blend traditional and contemporary themes. Many find their roots in the stone carvings of Great Zimbabwe, the age-old mythological beings of folklore, and in the natural rock formations of the country's landscape itself.

The rural population of Zimbabwe continues to make a wide variety of artistically designed articles for daily use. Carved wooden headrests, ornamented knives and gourds, baskets containing panels of carved wood, musical instruments, and a wide variety of earthenware pots are made throughout the countryside. The most striking shared feature of these objects is their rich, geometric decoration. Artists also continue to make wooden masks according to age-old designs. A number of wood-carvers have blended this traditional art form with Western themes.

An art gallery in Harare displays many fine modern **Shona sculptures** in an out- door garden.

A child probably made this **toy car from scraps of wire.** Wire art is growing in popularity in Zimbabwe and being shown in art galleries.

Children in Zimbabwe, as elsewhere in Africa, twist leftover wire from fencing projects into intricate toys with moving parts, such as cars and bicycles. Wire art has grown more sophisticated, and the National Gallery of Art in Bulawayo exhibits sculptures made by adults, entirely out of wire and other found materials, including bottle tops or tin cans. Dr. Yvonne Vera, the director of the gallery, said of the art, "It's a cross between an inventiveness, which comes out of a lack of material, and basic creativity which all of us share."

Literature, Drama, and Film

The people of Zimbabwe have a rich storytelling tradition that expresses itself in legends, epic poems, praise songs, and ballads that have been handed down orally for generations. In addition to traditional oral literary forms, there has been a flourishing market for published works in English, Ndebele, and Shona. Commercial firms and the government-backed Literature Bureau produce a wide range of publications. The Zimbabwe International Book Fair (ZIBF) is an independent association of professionals from the African literary community. ZIBF hosts an annual trade and cultural event.

Pre-independence authors have described the world of the white Rhodesian settlers. Doris Lessing's first novel, *The Grass Is Singing* (1950), depicts the hardship, isolation, and tragic racial tension experienced by a white woman farmer. Lessing, a world-famous author, was banned from the country until the 1980s for her outspoken opposition to the white minority government. The pre-independence black experience is the focus of Stanlake Samkange's *On Trial for My Country* (1966), which is about the seizure of land from Lobengula, and of Charles Mungoshi's novel *Waiting for the Rain* (1975). Dambudzo Marechera's collection of short stories *The House of Hunger*, which was first published in 1978, remains an honest expression of Zimbabwean frustration. Marechera is known for his stories dealing with psychological and social alienation.

> "The drought began. . . . There was not a green blade of grass left. There was not a green leaf of hope left; the drought had raised its great red hand and gathered them all and with one hot breath swept all the leaves into a red dot on the pencil-line of the horizon. . . . And the sun burnt each year to cinders. . . . "
>
> —Dambudzo Marechera, *The Writer's Grain*, 1978

Postindependence authors have produced a wealth of literature in the English language about the challenges of living in a changing society. Tsitsi Dangarembga's *Nervous Conditions*, winner of the 1988 Commonwealth Prize for Africa, is a novel about a girl torn between her traditional culture and her desire for an education at a British missionary school. Dangarembga is also a playwright and a filmmaker. Doris Lessing's *African Laughter, Four Trips to Zimbabwe* (1992) records her visits in the 1980s to the hopeful new nation of Zimbabwe. Alexander Kanengoni's novel *Echoing Silences* (1999) questions whether damage from war traumas can ever be repaired.

Peter Godwin and Alexandra Fuller are authors of British descent who write with sensitivity and intelligence about growing up during the end of white rule. Godwin's memoir is entitled *Mukiwa: A White Boy in Africa* (1996), and Fuller's is *Don't Let's Go to the Dogs Tonight* (2001). Yvonne Vera's dark, poetic novels are told from women's points of view. Her novel *The Stone Virgins* (2003) depicts the brutal experiences of two sisters during the atrocities in Matabeleland. Vera is also the director of the National Gallery of Art in Bulawayo. In 2004 Brian

Chikwava, a young writer and musician, won the Caine Prize for African Writing for his short story "Seventh Street Alchemy" about lively contemporary life in the heart of Harare.

About one hundred Zimbabwean theater groups are active in the country. The National Theatre Organization nurtures Zimbabwean playwrights, helps establish theater workshops, and coordinates dramatic activity throughout the country. English plays, including works by Shakespeare, are performed as well as traditional theater that is a blend of game, dance, and song. Plays may also combine cultures, mixing speech in English with songs in Shona and Ndebele. The popular musician Oliver Mtukudzi is also a playwright. He wrote and directed the lively musical *Was My Child*, which highlights the plight of street children.

Zimbabwean films cover a range of topics. The title of the popular 1990 movie *Jit* comes from Zimbabwean pop music called *jit-jive*. This uplifting film has a musical score that includes contributions from many of Zimbabwe's leading musicians. Doris Lessing's novel *The Grass Is Singing*, was made into a film in 1995. *Flame* (1996) is the first film to focus on Zimbabwe's women freedom fighters. *Everyone's Child* (1996) dramatizes the traditional African proverb "It takes a village to raise a child" as it follows the plight of two children whose parents die of AIDS. It was made by Tsitsi Dangarembga, author of *Nervous Conditions*. *Yellow Card* (2000) is a funny look at a teenage boy's love of life, girls, and soccer.

Music and Dance

Music is a constant presence in Zimbabwe. When music is for dancing, its style is flamboyant, and the *manyawi* (the spirit of expression and excitement) develops the pace of the tune. If, however, the music is for a solemn occasion, musicians hold back the tempo to create a serious mood. Many lyrics simply express everyday events. For example, a babysitter sings a nurse's song to a baby when its mother is working in the fields, or a midwife chants a presentation song when she gives a newborn baby to its father.

Marimbas are very popular instruments. Like the xylophone, a marimba is made of strips of wood that vary in length, which are attached to a soundboard. Musicians strike the strips with wooden hammers to produce the melody. Marimbas can vary considerably in size, which affects their pitch, and a group of these instruments may be played together as a band. The handheld mbira, sometimes called a thumb piano, works on a similar principle but is smaller. The sound is produced from iron rods fixed to a wooden soundboard. These rods are plucked with the thumb or forefinger to provide a melody. The most important musical instrument in Zimbabwe is the drum. Drums are made in a number of sizes to provide a variety of tones and pitches and are usually carved from solid blocks of wood with designs cut or burnt into them. Drum makers who maintain a traditional respect for nonhuman life ask the spirit of trees for permission to make drums from their wood.

Oliver Mtukudzi, called Tuku, is the best-selling songwriter and performer in Zimbabwe, having recorded more than forty albums over two decades. He combines several musical elements: a hard-driving rhythm from South Africa; the fast, Zimbabwean dance beat called jit; and gentler mbira rhythms. He draws his ideas from his community and sings about the difficulties of everyday life, often with a sense of humor. The nine-member band the Black Spirits accompanies Mtukudzi. Thomas Mapfumo, called the Lion of Zimbabwe and accompanied by his band the Blacks United, is another one of Zimbabwe's top musicians. He developed the musical style called *chimurenga*, which is committed to the struggle for human rights and Shona culture. It blends an electronic interpretation of mbira music with Western instruments. Mapfumo's lyrics encourage political and social justice. Both Mtukudzi and Mapfumo have international followings.

Oliver Mtukudzi performs at a festival in Seattle, Washington, in 2001.

Demonstrations of the local dances of Zimbabwe occur at Chapunga Park. It is a museum and artists' workshop near Harare. To learn more about Zimbabwe's cultural heritage go to www.vgsbooks.com for links.

Dance, accompanied by drumming, is ever present in Zimbabwe's villages and cities. Dance in Africa fulfills more functions than it usually does in the West. Besides being beautiful and expressive, it is a vital part of the community and is central to all gatherings, whether to celebrate the harvest or to welcome visiting politicians. Specific dances are preserved for generations and help provide cultural unity.

Many of the dances are spiritual or religious dances and are powerful expressions of the people's belief system. It is believed that dances are able to invoke the spirits of ancestors. Religious occasions, such as weddings and funerals, include stylized dancing as part of the rituals. Dances can go on for hours or even days.

Another category of dance, commemorative dance, is linked to political and historical events. The dances incorporate codes and symbols to help people remember the past, much as oral storytelling does. Social dances celebrate community, contributing to the general well-being, beauty, and order of the people and the cosmos. Dance clubs are popular for recreational dancing.

Western influence, the loss of kinship ties as people move to the cities, and the upheavals of war and economic turmoil have weakened the dance traditions of Zimbabwe. Nonetheless, dance continues to be an important force in society. Professional dance groups such as the National Dance Company preserve and perform traditional dances.

◐ Religion

More than 25 percent of the people of Zimbabwe are members of Christian churches. Christian missions provided Western-style education and health care for black Zimbabweans from the mid-1800s onward. Many of Zimbabwe's present leaders have Christian backgrounds. Robert Mugabe, for instance, was educated by the Jesuits (a Roman Catholic religious order) and is a practicing Catholic. Since independence, however, the growth of Christianity has slowed to a great extent.

About 50 percent of Zimbabwe's people practice syncretism (the combination of different beliefs) that, to various degrees, combines elements of local, traditional religious practices with Christian rituals. The Muslim (followers of Islam) community, mostly immigrants, makes up just 1 percent of the country's population.

Traditional religion continues to be widely practiced in rural areas. The Shona and the Ndebele share many religious customs and values. In Zimbabwe, religion is preserved and expressed in words, music, and dance from generation to generation. The central belief is in the existence of a spirit world. The power and vital life force of the invisible

The student art decorating the **Christian mission chapel in Cyrene**, Zimbabwe, has a wealth of distinctively indigenous details. This Christian mission, founded in 1939, is located 20 miles (32 km) from Bulawayo.

spirit world affects all of the visible, physical world. This belief is sometimes called animism.

There are five elements, from greater to lesser importance, in the animist belief system. They are God, called Mwari, the creator of all things; spirits of different kinds, both superhuman beings and the spirits of ancestors; humans living now and those about to be born; animals and plants; and all inanimate (nonliving) objects. These elements all relate to one another, each affecting the other. Because everything is connected to everything else, the collective good of the community is valued more highly than the individual alone.

It is believed that living people may communicate with the spirit world through the *masvikiro*, or spirit mediums. Music and dance plays a central role in contacting spirits. Spirit mediums may be extremely powerful forces in political and social events, as the woman who was the medium for the spirit Nehanda was during the First Chimurenga. The nganga, a spiritual healer, treats illness and detects the spiritual origin of illness too. Illnesses are considered to be caused by witchcraft, which upsets the harmony of the community. Often the nganga determines that a sacrifice, such as killing a goat, may be required to restore the balance.

Sports and Recreation

Sporting events attract large crowds in Zimbabwe. Cricket, originally an English game similar to baseball, is a popular sport. The highest level of play is international competitions called test matches. Zimbabwe has one of nine different national teams that play at this

Zimbabwean athlete **Kirsty Coventry** *(center)* brought home three Olympic medals from the 2004 Summer Olympics in Athens, Greece. Hundreds of fans and a traditional dancer *(right)* greeted her at Harare's main airport.

PRINCESS OF SPORT

Zimbabwe's Olympic swimmer Kirsty Coventry brought home three medals from the 2004 Summer Olympics in Athens, Greece. Her gold medal in the 200-meter backstroke was Zimbabwe's first Olympic gold medal. Coventry also won the silver in the 100-meter backstroke and the bronze in the individual medley, a swimming event combining the backstroke, breaststroke, butterfly stroke, and freestyle. She turned in African record-breaking times in all three events.

level. The country hosted the World Cricket Cup in 2004. Zimbabweans also love soccer, called football, and came in second in the Africa Cup of Nations in 2004.

Adventure sports such as white-water rafting, bungee jumping, and hot-air ballooning are enjoyed by visitors, especially around the Victoria Falls area. Zimbabwe's many excellent national parks offer safaris of all types, including walking, camping, and backpacking trips. Safaris were originally hunting expeditions. Modern large-game hunting requires special, expensive permits. Fishing is popular both for sport and for food.

Tsoro is a traditional Shona game. It is played by moving stones along rows of holes in the ground or on a board with carved holes and pieces. A version of this game, also known as *mankala,* is played all over Africa.

Food

Corn, the most common staple, is served in some shape or form at nearly every meal. Breakfast is usually cornmeal porridge, called *sadza,* served sweetened. Lunch might be a bowl of sadza with vegetables. Roasted corn on the cob makes an afternoon snack, and samp (hominy corn) and beans with grilled steak or chicken, if meat is available, is eaten for dinner.

Fruits and vegetables of all kinds thrive in Zimbabwe's warm climate. Pumpkin, yams, and spinach are native to the African continent. Corn, tomatoes, and peppers, originally from South America and introduced during trade with Portugal, are mixed with native vegetables to create side dishes, salads, and soups.

Peanuts, called groundnuts, are also native to Africa. Used in a variety of ways, they add flavor and protein to many dishes. The caterpillars of the Emperor moth, called mopane worms, are a traditional snack in Zimbabwe. Packed with protein and minerals, the caterpillars are a nutritious supplement to the rural diet.

SADZA/CORNMEAL PORRIDGE

Sadza is the basic food in Zimbabwe, as bread is in the West or rice in the East. Sadza is rolled into little balls and dipped into sauces and stews, depending upon what is available and what meal is being served. American tastes probably would prefer a sprinkle of salt in this recipe.

2 cups water   **1¼ cup white cornmeal**

1. Bring 1 cup water to a boil in a small saucepan. As the water heats, pour 1 cup water into a medium bowl. Slowly add ¾ cup `cornmeal to the water in the bowl, stirring constantly until the mixture has a pastelike consistency.
2. Carefully pour the cornmeal mixture from the bowl and into the boiling water in the saucepan, stirring to combine. Turn the heat to low and continue to stir the mixture, cooking for 4 or 5 minutes. Add the remaining cornmeal, and stir until the porridge thickens and pulls away from the sides of the pan.
3. Use a spatula to scrape the porridge into a lightly greased bowl. When it's cool enough to handle, shape the porridge into bite-sized balls.

Serve immediately.

THE ECONOMY

Zimbabwe had one of southern Africa's most successful economies at independence in 1980. The country has considerable natural resources—farmland, a temperate climate, minerals, and wild animals in beautiful settings. Zimbabwe also had a well-developed infrastructure (system of public works, such as roads). Agriculture was the leading factor in the economy, but the growth of service and industrial sectors overtook it in contributions to the gross domestic product (GDP—the amount of goods and services produced by a country in a year).

In the twenty-first century, Zimbabwe is in an economic crisis. Its involvement in the war in the Congo cost the country hundreds of millions of dollars. Ongoing haphazard farm seizures, violent elections, and poor government management have led to skyrocketing unemployment (70 percent) and inflation (500 percent). The overall GDP declined by 23 percent between 1997 and 2001 and continues downward. The AIDS epidemic drains the workforce. Farm production has decreased, foreign investment has plummeted (from $444 million in 1998 to $26 million in 2002), and tourism no longer brings in revenue. Electric power, fuel, and food are in short supply.

Land Resettlement

Despite Zimbabwe's well-developed agricultural sector and its diversity of farming products, most agricultural cultivation in the twenty-first century is subsistence farming, producing only the food to feed the farm family, without any left over for sale. After independence the most productive land remained in the hands of the white minority, who ran large commercial farms. These farms were crucial to the nation's economy as the source of exports, foreign exchange, crops, and jobs. The majority of black farmers remained poor peasants or worked as laborers on the commercial farms.

President Mugabe's government began a state-sponsored campaign to claim white-owned farmland in 2000. The land seizures were carried out by increasingly disorganized and violent groups of citizens. Nearly 300,000 black farmworkers were put out of work, and most were made homeless along with their families. Agricultural productivity declined sharply. Foreign investors pulled out, and without foreign money, Zimbabweans could not import fertilizer, spare parts, gasoline, and other supplies necessary for large-scale agriculture. The breakdown of law and order caused business confidence and tourism practically to disappear, increasing the economy's downward spiral.

Agriculture and Forestry

Zimbabwe's agricultural sector produces a variety of foods, cash crops, and livestock. About 66 percent of the workforce are small-scale farmers or farmworkers on commercial farms. Agriculture produces about 17 percent of the dwindling GDP.

Corn is the dietary staple food crop. The nation's principal cash crops for sale are tobacco, cotton, and sugar. Zimbabwe was the third largest source of tobacco in the world, producing 529 million pounds (240 million kilograms) in 2000, dropping to 154 million pounds (70 million kg) in 2003. Other crops are sorghum (a cereal grain), rice, barley, coffee, peanuts, soybeans, sunflowers, tea, beans, and potatoes. Fruit growers produce and export almost every kind of fruit from apples and pears to tropical fruits such as mangoes and papayas. Fresh flowers are also exported.

In the early 1990s, the annual production of beef supplied most of the domestic needs of Zimbabwe. After 2000, livestock started to suffer from lack of animal feed and loss of grazing lands due to drought. Unable to feed them, farmers sold their animals, and prices fell. The national herd of commercial beef cattle declined by almost half between 1999 and 2002.

Teakwood, which is used as support timber in mines and as crossbars on railway tracks, is grown in the forests of northwestern Zimbabwe.

Locally grown flowers are sold in a Harare market. Greenhouses growing most of the flowers that are sold to other countries are also concentrated near Harare. The main markets for Zimbawe's flowers are the Netherlands (86 percent) and South Africa (7 percent). The remaining 7 percent go to Australia, Far East nations, Germany, the United Kingdom, and the United States.

Mahogany from the southwest provides raw material for the furniture industry. Vast tracts of pine plantations were planted in the eastern districts under the colonial administration and the Mugabe government. The forest industry has made little progress, however, since whole areas of precious timber have been cut down for fuel.

Industry, Manufacturing, and Mining

In some ways, the economic sanctions that were imposed on the Rhodesian government in the 1960s and 1970s proved beneficial to independent Zimbabwe. Forced to become self-reliant, the Rhodesian regime made great strides in manufacturing import substitutes. After independence, Zimbabwe's raw materials and stable economy encouraged industrial development. In addition, taxes were low, a large workforce was available, and transportation and modern banking and financial services were efficient.

In the twenty-first century, industry produces 24 percent of the GDP. This includes manufacturing at 16 percent and mining at 2 percent. The outlook for the industrial sector of the economy looks bleak in the early 2000s. Lack of investor confidence due to the unstable economic and political climate, shortages of fuel and agricultural products, and a workforce diminished by AIDS and emigration have severely hindered industry.

A wide variety of industries has historically supplied consumer goods and goods for everyday domestic needs. Most foodstuffs are processed locally. Due to the decline in agricultural products, companies operate well below their capacity, however. Cement, fertilizers, glass, paper, rubber products, and textiles are all made in Zimbabwean factories. Surplus manufactured goods flow through Zimbabwe's export market, but exports have declined.

Leading exports have typically included tobacco, horticultural products, and gold. Cotton lint, textiles, footwear, ferroalloys (components of steel and cast iron, such as chromium, manganese, and silicon), and raw sugar are some of the other export commodities. Specialized items such as medical instruments and electronic

EXOTIC FARMING

Crocodiles and ostriches are farmed commercially in Zimbabwe for their skins, which are exported to be made into high-fashion leather goods such as shoes. Their meat is also eaten. This unusual kind of farming not only brings in substantial foreign currency but also has conservation benefits. Because crocodiles were once hunted almost to extinction, farmers are required to return a proportion of hatchlings to the wild. Ostriches are also restocked into areas where they once lived.

equipment are imported. Companies engaged in industry are under severe economic pressures, and hundreds of companies have closed in the twenty-first century.

Gold is the leading source of mining revenue in Zimbabwe but is dependent on the varying world gold price. The price of gold in the early 2000s has been depressed, and many gold mines in Zimbabwe have lost money or closed. Zimbabwe's mining industry also furnishes more than forty different minerals and metals. Nickel, used in making stainless steel, follows gold in bringing in export revenue. The country's deposits of chromite—from which chrome is made—are among the largest in the world. Zimbabwe's coal-mining business is well established at Hwange. Asbestos, copper, iron ore, lithium, silver, granite, limestone, phosphate rock, and tin are other mining resources. Significant reserves of the precious metal platinum, along with gemstones, including diamonds and emeralds, hold the potential to attract foreign investors to Zimbabwe. If the political climate improves, interest in exploiting these resources could aid in the recovery of the nation's economy.

Part-time mining activity along Zimbabwe's Great Dike brings in extra income to help families through tough economic times. Individuals sift through pans of sand and soil for gems and gold.

Service Sector

The service sector includes jobs in and revenue from education, health care, retail, trade, tourism, transportation, and government. Services average 59 percent of Zimbabwe's GDP.

Zimbabwe's tourist receipts in the mid-1990s—about $100 million annually—made tourism one of the economy's major industries. Visitors to Zimbabwe enjoyed the moderate climate, the beautiful scenery, friendly people, and the chance to see wild animals in the country's national parks. More than 2 million tourists visited the country in 1999. In 2000 tourist arrivals dropped 67 percent to about 700,000. The entire service industry suffers from this ongoing decline in tourism, from hotel workers to artisans. The loss of income also hurts the maintenance of national parks and the well-being of wild animals.

Zimbabwe's rail, land, and air transportation facilities upon independence were well established. After independence, much emphasis was given to the construction of roads to serve rural areas, which were neglected under the white-controlled government. Even though they are in need of considerable repair, these roads remain generally adequate. Zimbabwe has 11,394 miles (18,338 km) of highways, of which 5,401 miles (8,692 km) are paved.

Rail lines cover most of the country except for the region south of Lake Kariba. The government-owned National Railway of Zimbabwe connects with the South African rail system and the Mozambique ports of Maputo and Beira.

Air Zimbabwe, the national airline, has a monopoly on domestic routes. Several international and regional airlines fly into Harare, Bulawayo, and Victoria Falls. Air Zimbabwe also has international flights to Europe and many neighboring African countries.

Hydroelectric Power and Fuel

Zimbabwe ranks high among tropical-zone countries in the number of dams it has constructed. In nondrought years, hydroelectric power along with plentiful coal deposits supplies most of the country's energy needs. Dams also collect water during peak rainfall periods and store water for domestic and industrial uses in all the major population centers in Zimbabwe. In addition to the major dams, many smaller ones have been constructed on farms, at mines, and near villages throughout Zimbabwe.

Zimbabwe has no petroleum of its own and has suffered from a serious vehicle fuel shortage since 1999 because it lacks foreign currency to pay for imported fuel. The government increased fuel prices by 74 percent in 2001. In 2002 Zimbabwe struck a deal with Libya to supply petroleum in exchange for exports or land. A limited amount of petroleum comes into the landlocked country through a pipeline from the Mozambique port of Beira.

Foreign Debt, Black Market, and Crime

WORLD BANK AND THE IMF

The World Bank, an agency of the United Nations, has been operating since 1946. It is an international organization that lends money to member countries on long-term credit. It funds projects that it determines will help develop a country, such as irrigation, education, health, and housing. It also gives loans to try to persuade the government to adopt policies that help the economy, such as lower import tariffs (taxes) and efficient judicial (court) systems. The International Monetary Fund (IMF) is closely connected to the World Bank. The IMF offers policy advice and short-term loans to countries willing to change their economic policies. For instance, the IMF may insist that a country in financial difficulty take steps to reduce its budget deficit and inflation. These policies may cause initial economic hardships but are designed to create long-term economic stability.

Zimbabwe owes a lot of money—equaling 46 percent of its GDP—to lenders in other countries. In 2000 the World Bank placed the country on a "non-accrual status," meaning the nation had fallen behind on its repayments to the bank by more than six months. The IMF expelled Zimbabwe in 2003 because the government refused to cooperate in policy implementation and payments. Other international donors and lenders will only fund humanitarian work in Zimbabwe. Foreign business investors are unwilling to extend credit to the country.

As a result of its weak economy, Zimbabwe has a large black market, selling everything from gasoline to sugar. The term *parallel market*—referring to the unofficial economy, either legal or illegal—is sometimes used instead of *black market*. Exchange of money is commonly done unofficially on the parallel market because the Reserve Bank of Zimbabwe has fixed the value of the nation's money far higher than its actual worth. In the early 2000s, the official government rate was ZWD (Zimbabwe dollar) 825 per U.S.$1. But parallel market traders sell ZWD 5,000 for U.S.$1 to pay for goods and services available within the parallel market.

Zimbabwe's high unemployment and desperate economic circumstances have led to an increase in crime, including carjacking, street crime, and credit card fraud. Many women and youth turn to prostitution out of extreme poverty.

Catch up on the latest news from Zimbabwe. Visit www.vgsbooks.com for links to national and international news websites.

The Future

Robert Mugabe and his ZANU-PF party have dominated the country since 1980. Under his leadership, Zimbabwe of the twenty-first centry faces many challenges, including economic collapse, AIDS, famine, international isolation, land issues, political repression, and corrupt government.

In 2004 Robert Mugabe celebrated his eightieth birthday. If he chooses to retire before his presidential term ends, the constitution states that the person to succeed him will be chosen by the country's provincial governments. Political analysts say Mugabe likely would influence that choice and choose a successor from among his ZANU-PF political supporters. Otherwise, voters will have a chance to vote for president again in 2008.

If confidence in the government can be restored, possibly through free and fair elections in the future, the World Bank and foreign donor countries such as Britain, which have withdrawn their financial aid, would help the bankrupt country become economically self-sufficient again. Economic recovery is essential to tackling the AIDS pandemic. Other African countries have demonstrated that HIV/AIDS can be partially conquered through education, prevention, and medicine, which requires money and planning and coordination at all levels of society. The devastated farm sector will also need coordinated planning and many years to regain its health and again produce enough food to feed the nation as well as to produce income-generating export crops.

In the first few years of the 1980s, citizens of the new republic worked together to improve their country. In the twenty-first century, the people of Zimbabwe have not given up on the possibility of democratic change. Even in a climate of fear, many citizens have shown up at the voting booths to cast their ballots for an opposition voice in their government. In casting these votes, many citizens are demonstrating their optimism that Zimbabweans can once again make their country the jewel of Africa.

CA. 100,000 B.C. Ancient peoples live in prehistoric Zimbabwe.

CA. 18,000 B.C. Nomadic ancestors of the San people leave tools and other evidence of their Stone Age hunting and gathering societies.

CA. A.D. 900 Trade of precious metals from the southern African interior with Arab merchants on the Indian Ocean coast begins.

CA. 1000 People of the Shona language group migrate into Zimbabwe. The building of the stone city of Great Zimbabwe begins.

CA. 1400 Great Zimbabwe begins to decline. The Monomotapa kingdom arises.

1528 Portuguese traders begin trading in the interior of southern Africa, including the Monomotapa kingdom.

1541 The Portuguese establish the first European colony in southern Africa.

1690 The Rozvi group of the Changamire Empire drive the Portuguese out of their territory and begin to challenge the Monomotapa kingdom.

1839 Mzilikazi and his followers settle near the present-day city of Bulawayo and establish what comes to be called the Ndebele kingdom of Matabeleland.

CA. 1840 Lack of trade causes the Changamire Empire to decline.

1855 David Livingstone becomes the first British person to see Victoria Falls.

1859 Christian missionaries establish a mission and school at Inyati. Interest in southern Africa by European hunters, traders, and missionaries grows.

1888 Ndebele king Lobengula, son of Mzilikazi, is tricked by the British into signing an agreement granting them exclusive mineral rights.

1889 Cecil Rhodes obtains a charter from Queen Victoria to rule the lands of the Shona and the Ndebele through his British South Africa Company (BSAC).

1890 The Pioneer Column, two hundred British members of Rhodes's BSAC, arrives in Salisbury (modern Harare). The settlers are granted farm-land and mining rights by Rhodes without consulting the people living on the land.

1893 BSAC goes to war against the Ndebele. Lobengula flees BSAC forces.

1896 Ndebele and Shona unite against the white settlers in the First Chimurenga (war of liberation). They are defeated by the supe-rior weapons of the settlers.

1923 BSAC rule ends, and Southern Rhodesia (present-day Zimbabwe) is made a colony of the British Empire. It is self-governed by a white minority.

1932 Shona and Ndebele leaders form the African

National Congress of Southern Rhodesia to work toward
equality for blacks through legal means.

1953   The colonies of Southern Rhodesia, Northern Rhodesia, and
Nyasaland are joined in the Central African Federation. Black Africans
oppose this federation.

1955   Construction of the Kariba Dam on the Zambezi River begins.

1961   The Zimbabwe African People's Union (ZAPU), the first of the nationalist groups
to emerge in the 1960s, is formed by Joshua Nkomo.

1963   The Central African Federation is dissolved, as Great Britain gradually returns
self-government to its African colonies.

1965   Prime Minister Ian Smith announces a Unilateral Declaration of Independence from
Great Britain so the country, renamed Rhodesia, can maintain white minority rule.
International sanctions are imposed.

1972   A war against white rule, called the Second Chimurenga, intensifies. ZANU (formed by jailed
leader Robert Mugabe) and ZAPU guerrilla forces operate out of Zambia and Mozambique.

1980   Zimbabwe officially gains independence on April 18. Robert Mugabe and his ZANU-PF
Party win national elections.

1982   Prime Minister Mugabe removes Nkomo from government. The Shona Fifth Brigade carries
out a brutal "wiping away" of Ndebele in Matabeleland. Women are declared legal adults.

1987   Nkomo merges his party into Mugabe's ZANU-PF, and violence in Matabeleland ceases.
Mugabe changes the constitution to become executive president.

1998   Zimbabwe sends troops to the Democratic Republic of Congo. Zimbabweans demonstrate
against growing economic crisis with riots and strikes.

2000   Hundreds of white-owned farms are seized by government-sponsored war veterans and
squatters. Drought and disruption of agriculture cause food shortages. Despite violent repression, the Movement for Democratic Change Party wins 57 out of 120
elected seats in parliament.

2001   The World Bank, the IMF, and most western donors cut aid to Zimbabwe. Food shortages threaten famine.

2002   Troops withdraw from the Congo. Mugabe wins a presidential election widely con-
demned as unfair. Zimbabwe is suspended from the Commonwealth of Nations.

2003   A general strike is followed by arrests and violence. Zimbabwe pulls out of the
Commonwealth of Nations. HIV/AIDS prevalence among Zimbabwean adults is
estimated at 33 percent.

2004   Robert Mugabe celebrates his eightieth birthday. The UN estimates two-thirds
of Zimbabwe's population is dependent on foreign food aid. Zimbabwe hosts
the World Cricket Cup amidst protests of human rights abuses. White
Zimbabwean swimmer Kirsty Coventry wins Olympic gold, silver, and
bronze medals at the Summer Olympics in Athens, Greece.

COUNTRY NAME Republic of Zimbabwe

AREA 150,820 square miles (390,624 sq. km)

MAIN LANDFORMS Highveld, Middleveld, Lowveld, Eastern Highlands

HIGHEST POINT Mount Inyangani, 8,514 feet (2,595 m) above sea level

LOWEST POINT junction of the Lundi and Sabi rivers, 531 feet (162 m)

MAJOR RIVERS Zambezi, Limpopo, Sabi, Sanyati, Lundi

ANIMALS elephants, hippopotamuses, monkeys, rhinoceroses, aardvarks, aardwolves, bush babies, clawless otters, honey badgers, hyenas, pangolins, warthogs, cheetahs, leopards, lions, antelopes, buffalo, giraffes, wildebeests, zebras, crocodiles, lizards, snakes, canaries, cuckoos, eagles, finches, ostriches, robins, swallows

CAPITAL CITY Harare

OTHER MAJOR CITIES Bulawayo, Chitungwiza, Mutare

OFFICIAL LANGUAGE English

MONETARY UNIT Zimbabwean dollar (ZWD). 100 cents = 1 ZWD

Currency   Fast Facts

ZIMBABWEAN CURRENCY

The Zimbabwean dollar comes in notes of 5, 10, 20, 50, 100, 500, and 1,000 dollars. Coins have a value of 1, 5, 10, 20, and 50 cents, as well as 1 and 2 dollars. Constant soaring inflation causes exchange rates to fluctuate rapidly. Therefore, stable foreign currency, especially U.S. dollars and the South African rand, are in high demand. Official bank rates for the Zimbabwean dollar are fixed by the government at a rate higher than the real value, so foreign money is often exchanged on the parallel market. Due to the collapsing economy, counterfeit money is common.

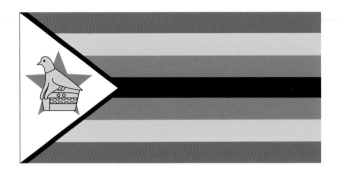

Zimbabwe adopted a new flag when it became an independent nation in 1980. Seven colored stripes run horizontally. Their colors are symbolic: green stands for agriculture, yellow for mineral wealth, red for the blood shed during the struggle for self-rule, and black for the ethnic majority of the population. A white triangle, symbolizing a peaceful path ahead, is on the left side of the flag. The triangle bears a yellow Great Zimbabwe Bird with a red star behind it. The soapstone bird carving was found among the ruins of Great Zimbabwe and has become a symbol of the nation. The red star stands for internationalism as well as the goals of the ruling government.

Zimbabwe adopted its national anthem in 1994. Solomon Mutswairo wrote the words, and Fred L. Changundega contributed the music.

Blessed Be the Land of Zimbabwe
O lift high the banner, the flag of Zimbabwe
The symbol of freedom proclaiming victory;
We praise our heroes' sacrifice,
And vow to keep our land from foes;
And may the Almighty protect and bless our land.

O lovely Zimbabwe, so wondrously adorned
With mountains, and rivers cascading, flowing free;
May rain abound, and fertile fields;
May we be fed, our labour blessed;
And may the Almighty protect and bless our land.

O God, we beseech thee to bless our native land;
The land of our fathers bestowed upon us all;
From Zambezi to Limpopo
May leaders be exemplary;
And may the Almighty protect and bless our land.

For a link where you can listen to Zimbabwe's national anthem, go to www.vgsbooks.com.

Famous People

ANDREW FLOWER (b. 1968) Andrew "Andy" Flower is one of the world's best cricket players. Born in Cape Town, South Africa, he moved with his family to Harare when he was ten, and he has played for Zimbabwe since 1988. In the 2003 World Cup, he (a white Zimbabwean) and his team-mate Henry Olonga (a black Zimbabwean) wore black armbands at the start of the first match, mourning, they said, "the death of democracy in our beloved Zimbabwe."

DORIS LESSING (b. 1919) Born in Persia (modern-day Iran), Lessing arrived in Southern Rhodesia (Zimbabwe) at age five, the child of British parents. When she was thirty, she moved to England and became a writer. Because of her outspoken opposition to white minority rule in Southern Rhodesia, she was declared a Prohibited Immigrant by its white government and not allowed to return until the 1980s. Several of her published works draw on her African experiences, including her first novel, *The Grass Is Singing.* She has been awarded many international prizes and been nominated for the Nobel Prize for Literature.

LOBENGULA (CA. 1836–1894) Lobengula was the leader of the Ndebele people and king of Matabeleland. In 1870 he took over from his father Mzilikazi, a Zulu king, who had settled the area. Lobengula tried to stop European colonizers. In 1888, however, under pressure from Cecil Rhodes, he gave up his mineral rights in exchange for a small payment. When British settlers began appearing, Lobengula rallied his people and in 1893 attacked the British. The results were disastrous for the Ndebele, and Lobengula died while fleeing north.

DAMBUDZO MARECHERA (1952–1987) Marechera was born in Vengere Township. This poet and novelist has been called Zimbabwe's most controversial writer. Literature, he said, "unhinges the world and churns up people's minds." His writing deals with psychological and social isolation. The University of Rhodesia expelled him for participating in student protests for independence. He later attended Oxford University in England on a scholarship. Marechera's collection of stories, *The House of Hunger,* was awarded the Guardian Fiction Prize in 1979. He published little else, but he and this book are considered among Zimbabwe's literary best.

ROBERT MUGABE (b. 1924) Born at Kutama Mission near Harare and raised and educated as a Roman Catholic, Mugabe became a hero of African nationalism. He founded the Zimbabwe African National Union (ZANU) in 1963. During the years he was jailed, without trial (1964–1974), he earned four college degrees, for a total of seven, mostly in economics and law. A guerrilla leader in the war for independence, he became independent Zimbabwe's first prime minister and chose a path of reconciliation. Over time, he consolidated power, brutally cracked down on opposition, and became increasingly autocratic. He was reelected in 2002 in a campaign marked by charges of election fraud.

NEHANDA (CA. 1000) Nehanda is one of the *mhondoro*, or great ancestor spirits, of the Shona people. Oral history records that Nehanda was a member of the first Shona family to arrive on the Zimbabwe plains. She died before they crossed the Zambezi River, but her spirit entered a medium who parted the waters so the immigrants could cross safely. According to legend, in 1896, during the First Chimurenga, Nehanda's spirit took possession of a medium and encouraged her people to resist the white settlers. The medium—named Charwe but referred to by her spirit name Nehanda—was hung by the British in 1897. Nehanda remains Zimbabwe's greatest heroine.

AGNES NYANHONGO (b. 1960) Agnes Nyanhongo was born in Nyanga. Her father, Claude Nyanhongo, was one of the sculptors from the work-shop that began in the late 1950s in Harare's National Gallery. He taught his daughter sculpting basics, and she has become one of the finest and most collected contemporary sculptors. She specializes in sculpting women of strength, grace, and dignity. In 2003 her work was included in an international sculpture exhibition tour titled In Praise of Women.

IAN SMITH (b. 1919) Smith was born in Selukwe, Rhodesia (Shurugwi, Zimbabwe, in modern times), the son of a wealthy Scottish father. He was a fighter pilot in the British Royal Air Force during World War II. He led the white supremacist Rhodesian Front (RF), taking office as prime minister in 1964. In 1965 he declared Rhodesia independent from Great Britain. Guerrilla war was waged against his government throughout the 1970s until, in 1980, the independent nation of Zimbabwe was declared. Smith became the leader of the opposition in Zimbabwe's parliament, but his party disintegrated. He retired in 1988 and returned to farming. In the 2002 elections, he said he supported the Movement for Democratic Change party.

MORGAN TSVANGIRAI (b. 1952) The eldest son of a bricklayer, Tsvangirai was born in Buhera, in eastern Zimbabwe. He worked as a miner and became the leader of the Zimbabwe Congress of Trade Unions. In 1999 he helped form the MDC. Supported by younger Zimbabweans, especially urban workers, Tsvangirai is the most effective opposition leader in Zimbabwe. He had been arrested and accused of attempting to assassinate Mugabe before the 2002 election, but he was acquitted by Zimbabwe's Supreme Court in 2004.

YVONNE VERA (b. 1964) Vera is one of Zimbabwe's best-known authors. She was born in Bulawayo and received a Ph.D. in English from York University in Canada. The author of short stories and novels, she won the Commonwealth Writers Prize (Africa Region) in 1997 for *Under the Tongue*. Vera's dense poetic prose expresses the trauma of war, which also celebrates love. As director of the National Gallery in Bulawayo, Vera develops exhibits that reflect real people's lives.

Note: In 2004, the U.S. Department of State issued a Travel Warning to Americans stating, "Zimbabwe is in the midst of political, economic and humanitarian crisis with serious implications for the security situation in the country." For updates, go to www.vgsbooks.com for a link.

BULAWAYO Zimbabwe's second-largest city is full of history. Old Bulawayo (Department of National Museums & Monuments) British colonial architecture still graces tree-lined streets. The famous Museum of Natural History displays Zimbabwe's natural and cultural history.

GREAT ZIMBABWE Great Zimbabwe National Monument is in the countryside, south of the city of Masvingo. Visitors can tour the second largest stone ruins in Africa (after the pyramids in Egypt). At the site is also a village that reconstructs what life was like for people who lived in the city.

HARARE Harare is the capital city of Zimbabwe and the center of commerce and government. Colonial-era buildings, including the parliament buildings, mix with modern architecture. The Mbare market is a busy African marketplace that sells everything from carvings to herbal remedies. The National Gallery includes world-renowned sculpture, created in the gallery's African sculpture workshop.

HWANGE NATIONAL PARK At the edge of the Kalahari Desert, this is Zimbabwe's largest park and has the most wildlife. Human-made watering holes allow wildlife to live through the dry season. Lions and other predators (meat eaters) are seen as well as large herds of elephants, zebras, antelopes, and buffalo, all amidst magnificent scenery.

MANA POOLS NATIONAL PARK Mana Pools is located south of the Zambezi River. This is one of the last places on earth where it is possible to see the endangered black rhinoceros. Crocodiles and hippopotamuses also live in and around the Zambezi River. Visitors must always be careful of wild animals. Despite their looks, hippos aggressively defending their territory kill more people every year than any other animal in Africa.

MATAPOS NATIONAL PARK Balancing granite boulders, prehistoric rock paintings, and rhinoceroses are the main features of this park south of Bulawayo. Cecil Rhodes is buried at a site called View of the World. The Ndebele sacred rain shrine is in a rock cleft of the Matopo Hills.

VICTORIA FALLS Located at the Zambian border, the falls are one of the most astonishing sights in all of Africa. Many adventure sports are available there, including bungee jumping from the Victoria Falls bridge.

animism: a religious practice of spirit worship. Spirit (conscious life) is believed to inhabit natural objects, natural events (such as storms and lightning), and human ancestors.

Bantu: a family of languages spoken in central and southern Africa; a member of any group of African peoples who speak these languages. Bantu means "people."

Chimurenga: a war of liberation

colony: a territory governed by a distant nation and inhabited in part by settlers from the nation

gross domestic product (GDP): the value of the goods and services produced by a country over a period of time, such as a year

guerrillas: small groups of fighters who operate independently, engaging in non-traditional warfare

hunter-gatherers: people who survive by hunting animals and gathering wild plants for food

hydroelectric power: electricity produced by the power of rushing water. Dams are built on rivers in order to create hydroelectric power stations.

irrigation: a system of supplying water to agricultural fields using canals, pipes, reservoirs, and other devices

literacy: the ability to read and write

nationalist: a member of a political party or group characterized by feelings of loyalty or patriotism toward its nation and for promoting a national culture and national interests

nganga: a traditional spiritual healer who treats physical illnesses

patrilineal: tracing family descent through the father and his male ancestors. The Shona and Ndebele people of Zimbabwe have patrilineal societies.

safari: means "we go" in Swahili, a language originating in Africa. In Zimbabwe, individuals may particpate in safaris—usually to observe animals or birds—on foot, by horseback or elephant, or on boats or rafts.

sanctions: an economic act, such as prohibiting trade, usually taken by several nations together to try to force another nation violating international law to reform

Southern Hemisphere: the half of the earth that is south of the equator (the halfway point between the North Pole and South Pole)

subsistence farming: a system of farming that produces only enough or not quite enough food necessary to feed the farm family, without any left over for sale

syncretism: the combination of different forms of spiritual beliefs or practices

veld: an Afrikaans word meaning "plain," an open grassland with scattered trees and shrubs

white supremacy: a belief that the white race is inherently superior to the black race and therefore should have more power in all realms of life

Selected Bibliography

***Africa South of the Sahara 2003.* London: Europa Publications, 2002.**
This annual guide focuses on the modern history and economy of Zimbabwe and other southern African countries and has a statistical survey of various factors, including population, health, agriculture, trade, education, and more.

Blair, David. *Degrees in Violence: Robert Mugabe and the Struggle for Power in Zimbabwe.* London: Continuum, 2002.
Blair was a foreign correspondent in Zimbabwe from 1999 to 2001. This book records his experience of the events of that period, including election rallies, farm invasions, food riots, and interviews with Zimbabweans from all walks of life.

Chan, Stephen. *Robert Mugabe: A Life of Power and Violence.* Ann Arbor: University of Michigan Press, 2003.
Chan is a professor of international relations in London. He seeks to explain Mugabe's rule as it went from the hopeful times of postindependence to the desperate measures of the early twenty-first century.

Chinula, Tione, and Vincent Talbot. *Zimbabwe.* Victoria, Australia: Lonely Planet, 2002.
This useful travel guidebook to Zimbabwe includes background information on history and politics, as well as the usual information about how to get around the country and what to see. The informative sections on safaris and wildlife are accompanied by vivid color photographs.

Courlander, Harold. *A Treasury of African Folklore.* New York: Crown Publishers, 1975.
This collection of the oral literature, myths, legends, sayings, and humor illuminates the human experience of African peoples. Explanatory essays set the tales in their cultural contexts. The section on the literary tradition of the southern Bantu includes some of the groups of Zimbabwe.

Dugard, Martin. *Into Africa: The Epic Adventures of Stanley and Livingstone.* New York: Doubleday, 2003.
This entertaining book focuses on David Livingstone's 1866 expedition, which vanished while looking for the source of the Nile, and journalist Henry Stanley's efforts to find it. It also recounts Livingstone's earlier travels on the Zambezi River that led him to Victoria Falls.

***The Economist.* 2004.**
http://www.economist.com (February 16, 2004)
This weekly British magazine, available on-line or in print editions, provides excellent in-depth coverage of international news, including Zimbabwe's economic and political news.

Lessing, Doris. *African Laughter: Four Visits to Zimbabwe.* New York: HarperCollins, 1992.
In the 1980s, after an exile of twenty-five years, Lessing, an author of British heritage, returned to the country she had grown up in. This book records what she found in the newly independent country in very readable, human terms, from conversations with white farmers and black poets to observations about everything from spirits to AIDS.

Mann, Kenny. *Monomotapa, Zulu, Basuto: Southern Africa.* **Parsippany, NJ: Dillon Press, 1996.**
This title includes information on Zimbabwean cultures. It is part of the African Kingdoms of the Past series, which looks at African cultures from the earliest times through their encounters with European cultures.

Meredith, Martin. *Our Votes, Our Guns: Robert Mugabe and the Tragedy of Zimbabwe.* **Cambridge, MA: Public Affairs, 2002.**
The author was a journalist and then a scholar and author on African affairs. He pieces together the story of what changed Mugabe from a visionary leader to a dictator.

Palmer, Robin, and Isobel Birch. *Zimbabwe: A Land Divided.* **Oxford, UK: Oxfam, 1992.**
Oxfam is an international aid organization. Its Country Profiles series is designed to look at international social, economic, and environmental issues, and especially to focus on the real lives of ordinary people. This book from the series examines the first decade of Zimbabwe's independence.

Population Reference Bureau. October 20, 2003.
http://www.prb.org **(March 2004)**
PRB provides demographics on Zimbabwe's population, health, environment, employment, family planning, and more.

Staunton, Irene, comp. and ed. *Mothers of the Revolution: The War Experiences of Thirty Zimbabwean Women.* **Bloomington: Indiana University Press, 1991.**
Interviews with mostly rural women in Zimbabwe reveal how they were affected by and involved in the 1970s' war for independence. The women talk personally of courage, endurance, and humor, as well as fear, violence, greed, and need.

U.S. Department of State, Bureau of African Affairs. *Background Notes: Zimbabwe.* **Washington, D.C.: U.S. Government Printing Office, 2001.**
This is a brief overview of the statistics, people, history, government, economics, and foreign relations of Zimbabwe.

Welsh Asante, Kariamu. *Zimbabwe Dance: Rhythmic Forces, Ancestral Voices—An Aesthetic Analysis.* **Trenton, NJ: Africa World Press, 2000.**
Dance is inseparable from traditional society in Zimbabwe. The author, a professor who teaches African dance, examines in depth two Zimbabwean dances, one Shona, the other Ndebele, and shows how their music and rhythm and symbols reflect and create a distinctive African world view.

The World Factbook. August 1, 2003.
http://www.odci.gov/cia/publications/factbook/geos/zi.html **(March 2004)**
This site of the CIA (the U.S. Central Intelligence Agency) provides ample facts and figures on Zimbabwean geography, government, economy, communications, transportation, and transnational issues.

African Studies Center at the University of Pennsylvania. *Zimbabwe Page.*
http://www.sas.upenn.edu/African_Studies/Country_Specific/Zimbabwe.html
This excellent site offers links to a wide range of sites featuring Zimbabwe's music, language, stamps and money, embassies, and newspapers. The mission statement of the center states that it has "a commitment to a broad, integrated approach to the study of African people, their institutions, and the wider world where they now reside."

BBC News.
http://news.bbc.co.uk
The World Edition of the BBC (British Broadcasting Corporation) News is updated throughout the day, every day. The BBC is a great resource for up-to-date comprehensive news coverage of Zimbabwe.

Cornell, Kari A., and Peter Thomas. *Cooking the Southern African Way.* **Minneapolis: Lerner Publications Company, 2005.**
This cultural cookbook looks at the land, people, traditions, cultures, and foods of the diverse nations of southern Africa, including Zimbabwe.

Dangarembga, Tsitsi. *Nervous Conditions.* **New York: Seal Press, 1988.**
This novel tells the story of Tambu, a teenager growing up in Rhodesia (present-day Zimbabwe) in the 1960s. She hopes to escape her poor rural community by getting a British-style education at a mission school. As she confronts the limitations both of colonial rule and of the traditional role of women, she sadly and painfully moves away from her cultural heritage.

Fuller, Alexandra. *Don't Let's Go to the Dogs Tonight: An African Childhood.* **New York: Random House, 2001.**
Fuller, a child of British settlers in Rhodesia, grew up during Zimbabwe's war for independence in a place where even children learned how to handle guns. Told with a young person's openness, this memoir captures the author's love for and conflict over her tormented homeland and her white supremacist parents.

Godwin, Peter. *Mukiwa: A White Boy in Africa.* **New York: Atlantic Monthly Press, 1996.**
Godwin writes with affection of being a boy in Zimbabwe's Eastern Highlands. As he grows up, he witnesses the violence and confusion of the collapsing colony. Though he supported independence, he found himself fulfilling his national service as a policeman in Matabeleland. Later, as a journalist, he covered the Fifth Brigade atrocities there. This is a balanced, informative, and fascinating book.

Maraire, J. Nozipo Nkosana. *Zenzele: A Letter for My Daughter.* **New York: Crown Publishers, 1996.**
Though fictionalized, this book provides a social history of Zimbabwe. It is written in the form of a Zimbabwean mother's letter to her daughter in America. The mother writes of her life as a traditional woman and depicts the tension between her way of life and the liberated, Western-influenced life of her daughter. Like a traditional village storyteller, she weaves personal stories with political insight.

Further Reading and Websites

McCall Smith, Alexander. *Tears of the Giraffe.* **New York: Anchor Books, 2000.**
Second in the popular No. 1 Ladies' Detective Agency series, written by an author who grew up in Zimbabwe, this amusing novel gives insight into the culture of a peaceful and prosperous southern African nation, which Zimbabwe once was. The likable heroine of the series, detective Precious Ramotswe, lives and works in Botswana but crosses the border into Zimbabwe in this novel.

Parker, Linda J. *The San of Africa.* **Minneapolis: Lerner Publications Company, 2002.**
This title is part of the First Peoples series. It describes the modern and traditional ways of life of the San people, the original inhabitants of southern Africa, and their struggles to live in the modern world.

Rogers, Barbara Radcliffe, and Stillman D. Rogers. *Zimbabwe.* **New York: Children's Press, 2002.**
This well-written book is part of the illustrated Enchantment of the World series.

Staunton, Irene, ed. *Writing Still: New Stories from Zimbabwe.* **Harare, Zimbabwe: Weaver Press, 2004.**
Twenty-three contemporary stories go to the heart of everyday realities of ordinary Zimbabweans. Some of Zimbabwe's best writers are represented in this anthology, including Brian Chikwava, Alexandra Fuller, and Charles Mungoshi.

Tucker, Neely. *Love in the Driest Season: A Family Memoir.* **New York: Crown Publishers, 2004.**
A firsthand account of the effect of AIDS on children, written by an American journalist who adopted an abandoned AIDS orphan while living in Zimbabwe. Tucker tells a personal story but gives ample coverage to the complex political and social circumstances surrounding the adoption.

Van Wyk, Gary, and Robert Johnson. *Shona.* **New York: Rosen, 1997.**
A title in the Heritage Library of African Peoples series, this book explores the history and culture of the Shona people, who make up about 75 percent of the population of Zimbabwe.

vgsbooks.com
http://www.vgsbooks.com
Visit vgsbooks.com, the homepage of the Visual Geography Series®. You can get linked to all sorts of useful on-line information, including geographical, historical, demographic, cultural, and economic websites. The vgsbooks.com site is a great resource for late-breaking news and statistics.

Captions for photos appearing on cover and chapter openers:

Cover: The local name for spectacular Victoria Falls is Mosi-oa-Tunya, meaning "smoke that thunders."

pp. 4–5 Workers in Hwange, Zimbabwe, harvest corn.

pp. 8–9 Stacks of boulders, or balancing rocks, are such a common sight in some parts of Zimbabwe that they appear on the nation's currency.

pp. 20–21 Prehistoric Zimbabweans painted hunting scenes on the walls of Silozwane Cave near Matopos National Park. The region was designated a UNESCO World Heritage site in 2004.

pp. 36–37 Three young women in the Mutasa region of Zimbabwe walk home from school.

pp. 46–47 Paintings and sculptures from Zimbabwe are displayed in a spacious exhibit hall at the National Gallery of Zimbabwe in Harare.

pp. 58–59 A rural village's communal harvest of corn is stored on a platform *(right)* to dry it. In the early twenty-first century, the UN World Food Programme projected annual harvests of less than half of what is needed to feed everyone in the country.